W9-BZV-132

POPE FRANCIS

The Courage to Be Happy

POPE FRANCIS

The Courage to Be Happy

*The Pope Speaks
to the Youth of the World*

Edited by Robert Ellsberg

ORBIS BOOKS
Maryknoll, New York 10545

ORBIS BOOKS
Maryknoll, New York 10545

Fathers and Brothers
MARYKNOLL

Founded in 1970, Orbis Books endeavors to publish works that enlighten the mind, nourish the spirit, and challenge the conscience. The publishing arm of the Maryknoll Fathers and Brothers, Orbis seeks to explore the global dimensions of the Christian faith and mission, to invite dialogue with diverse cultures and religious traditions, and to serve the cause of reconciliation and peace. The books published reflect the views of their authors and do not represent the official position of the Maryknoll Society. To learn more about Maryknoll and Orbis Books, please visit our website at www.maryknollsociety.org.

Copyright © 2018 by Editrice Libreria Vaticana

Published by Orbis Books, Box 302, Maryknoll, NY 10545-0302, in collaboration with Editrice Libreria Vaticana.

All rights reserved.

No part of this publication may be reproduced or transmitted in any form or by any means, electronic or mechanical, including photocopying, recording, or any information storage or retrieval system, without prior permission in writing from the publisher.

Queries regarding rights and permissions should be addressed to: Orbis Books, P.O. Box 302, Maryknoll, NY 10545-0302.

Manufactured in the United States of America

Library of Congress Cataloging-in-Publication Data

Names: Francis, Pope, 1936– author. | Ellsberg, Robert, 1955– editor.
Title: The courage to be happy : Pope Francis speaks to the youth of the
   world / edited by Robert Ellsberg.
Description: Maryknoll : Orbis Books, 2018.
Identifiers: LCCN 2017042081 | ISBN 9781626982727 (pbk.)
Subjects: LCSH: Church work with youth—Catholic Church. | World Youth Day
   (Assembly) | Catholic youth—Religious life.
Classification: LCC BX2347.8.Y7 F73413 2018 | DDC 252/.02—dc23 LC record
available at https://lccn.loc.gov/2017042081

Contents

WORLD YOUTH DAYS

APOSTOLIC JOURNEY TO BRAZIL
XXVIII WORLD YOUTH DAY, 2013

YOUTH DAY MESSAGES

FINAL REFLECTIONS
Looking Back, Looking Ahead

Introduction

By Father Thomas Rosica, CSB

On January 13, 2017, Pope Francis addressed a letter to the young people of the world. The occasion was the presentation of the Preparatory Document for the Synod of Bishops scheduled to take place in Rome in October 2018 under the theme, "Young People, the Faith, and Vocational Discernment." In his letter, the Holy Father reminded young people that they are the center of attention for the entire synodal process. The synod is to be about them! He reminded them that "a better world can be built also as a result of your efforts, your desire to change and your generosity."

> Do not be afraid to listen to the Spirit who proposes bold choices; do not delay when your conscience asks you to take risks in following the Master. The Church also wishes to listen to your voice, your sensitivities, and your faith; even your doubts and your criticism. Make your voice heard, let it resonate in communities and let it be heard by your shepherds of souls. Saint Benedict urged the abbots

to consult, even the young, before any important decision, because "the Lord often reveals to the younger what is best."

Thus began the journey to the October 2018 Synod and to the next World Youth Day set for Panama in 2019. For the next few years, all eyes and ears will be on young people! For this journey, I can think of no better companion than this brilliant, comprehensive collection of texts, reflections, homilies and addresses by Pope Francis. *The Courage to Be Happy* is not only a goldmine for young people but also a must read for anyone accompanying youth and young adults in the Church and the world today.

In these pages the reader will discover the vital connection that Pope Francis has established with young people throughout the world. He is truly a shepherd with the smell of the sheep; a pastor who listens carefully to the spoken and unspoken words of the young people he encounters around the world; a father who embraces those on the geographical and existential peripheries of humanity; and a grandfather who never fails to remind the young to build intergenerational bridges.

While Pope Francis made his world debut on the Vatican loggia the night of March 13, 2013, it was four months later in the streets of Rio de Janeiro and on Copacabana Beach that young people throughout the world discovered that this pope rocks! Many say that it was during Brazil's World Youth Day 2013 that the pope truly came into his own. In a vigil the night before the final Mass on Copacabana Beach, the Argentine pontiff asked the assembled youth to be "actors of change."

"The Church needs you, your enthusiasm, your creativity and the joy that is so characteristic of you," he told the huge throng, hundreds of thousands of whom had slept overnight on the beach. In the simple, evangelical, and radical style that has characterized his pontificate, Francis made an appeal to pilgrims to return to their home countries and revitalize the Catholic Church. He urged his young followers to be more active in their faith by reaching out "to the fringes of society, even to those who seem farthest away, most indifferent." An avid football fan, Pope Francis told his audience: "Jesus offers us something bigger than the World Cup!"

Three years later, Pope Francis traveled to Poland in July 2016 for World Youth Day in the very city where these great events were conceived in the mind and heart of the young priest and bishop, Karol Wojtyla, who would become Pope John Paul II. It was a challenging journey laden with layers of history and memory for millions of young people who claim to be part of the "John Paul II Generation." Whereas the Polish pontiff—now a saint—gave the Church the beautiful devotion and spirituality of Divine Mercy, Pope Francis crystallized the teaching of mercy as the central theme of his Petrine ministry and taught young people how to put that mercy into practice each day. God alone knows how many young people, how many sick, suffering, and handicapped persons Pope Francis stopped to touch and bless in the streets of Kraków. He embraced them and loved them. Those who took part in that great celebration of faith and Catholic life in Kraków would never be the same. They had traveled to Kraków as pilgrims. They were sent forth as missionary disciples to share what they had seen and heard.

World Youth Days have been a part of my life for more than twenty years. The body of teaching emerging from each international celebration offers to the Church a brilliant catechesis and teaching for all involved with young adults. At times, I have wondered about the density of the papal texts that seem to speak much more to adults than to young people. No doubt the Holy Spirit works through those texts as well, but the relative inaccessibility of previous texts was at times a challenge. During World Youth Day 2016 in Kraków, in contrast, I had no concerns whatsoever about the clarity of the texts and their ability to reach their target audience. The pope's words spoke powerfully, directly, and clearly to the youth of the world.

What emerges in each of the pope's addresses and talks is the image of an elderly person who has been young for a long time, a man who is truly evergreen, one who, despite his advanced age, remains deeply in touch with his times and the struggles of young people today.

On the eve of Palm Sunday in April 2017, Pope Francis gathered with several thousand teenagers and young adults for an evening prayer vigil at Saint Mary Major Basilica in downtown Rome. I was an eyewitness to the magic of that celebration! Officially launching the preparation for the 2018 Synod of Bishops and for World Youth Day 2019 in Panama, Francis gave young people several missions: to ask their grandparents what their dreams were; to work to make those dreams reality; and to let their bishops and the pope himself know what they need from the Church. Later, returning to his appeal that they speak to their grandparents, the pope said, "I don't know if it will be me, but the pope will be in Panama and he will ask you, 'Did you speak with your elders?'"

The Church could hold a synod involving Catholic youth active in parish life or Catholic organizations and lay movements. But Pope Francis said that is not what the Church or young people need. "This is the synod of young people and we want to hear all of them," including, he said, young people who have moved away from the Church or are questioning the existence of God. "Every young person has something to say to others, something to say to the adults, to the priests, sisters, bishops, and the pope. We all need to hear you."

I write these words of introduction in the afterglow of a wonderful, nationally televised forum of young adults across Canada who gathered together in early October 2017 to respond to the pope's desire that they speak out about their own lives, journeys, hopes and dreams, doubts and fears, concerns and questions. Pope Francis joined us through a special video link from the Vatican. His words and passion stirred each of us:

> I ask you, therefore, not to let the world be ruined by those without scruples, who think only about exploiting it and destroying it. I invite you to flood the places where you live with the joy and enthusiasm typical of your youthful age, to irrigate the world and history with the joy that comes from the Gospel, from having met a Person: Jesus, who has enthralled you and has drawn you to be with him.

The title of this collection, *The Courage to Be Happy*, beautifully sums up Pope Francis's mission and ministry to young people around the world. "God has placed in the heart of every man and woman an irrepressible desire for happiness, for fulfillment," the Holy Father says. "Dear young men and women, in Christ you find fulfilled your every desire for goodness and happiness. He alone can satisfy your deepest longings, which are so often clouded by deceptive worldly promises."

"Dear young friends," he continues, "in a culture of relativism and the ephemeral, many preach the importance of 'enjoying' the moment. They say that it is not worth making a life-long commitment, making a definitive decision, 'forever,' because we do not know what tomorrow will bring. I ask you, instead, to be revolutionaries, I ask you to swim against the tide; yes, I am asking you to rebel against this culture that sees everything as temporary and that ultimately believes you are incapable of responsibility, that believes you are incapable of true love."

May this wonderful collection of Pope Francis's reflections stir up in the hearts of everyone who reads it the desire to become a missionary disciple, a lover of mercy and truth, a doer of justice and charity, and a bearer of gospel joy that are the hallmarks of this octogenarian pope who is so youthful in mind and heart.

FR. THOMAS ROSICA, a priest of the Congregation of St. Basil, was ordained in 1986. He served as National Director and Chief Executive Officer of World Youth Day 2002 in Canada, and served from 2003 to 2017 as the Canadian National Coordinator for World Youth Days. In 2003 he founded Salt and Light Catholic Media Foundation and Television Network in Canada, the first fruit of World Youth Day in that country. He has also served as English language assistant to the Holy See Press Office.

DEAR YOUNG PEOPLE

Greetings

I see that there are large numbers of young people in the square. There you are! I say to you: Carry this certainty ahead: the Lord is alive and walks beside you through life. This is your mission! Carry this hope onwards. May you be anchored to this hope, this anchor that is in heaven; hold the rope firmly, be anchored and carry hope forward. You, witnesses of Jesus, pass on the witness that Jesus is alive and this will give us hope, it will give hope to this world, which has aged somewhat because of wars, because of evil, and because of sin. Press on, young people!

—*General Audience, April 3, 2013*

In the square I have seen that there are many young people here...I ask you, who are just setting out on your journey through life: Have you thought about the talents that God has given you? Have you thought of how you can put them at the service of others? Do not bury your talents! Set your stakes on high ideals, the ideals that enlarge the heart, the ideals of service that make your talents fruitful. Life is not given to us to be jealously guarded for ourselves; it is given to us so that we may give it in turn. Dear young people, have a deep spirit! Do not be afraid to dream of great things!

—*General Audience, April 24, 2013*

Yesterday we celebrated the liturgical feast of Saint Catherine of Siena, patroness of Italy and Europe. Dear young people, may you learn from her to live with the upright conscience of one who does not give in to human compromise.

—*General Audience, April 30, 2014*

Dear young people, be brave! Respond to the love of God with enthusiasm, as beloved children; respond with trust when you return to the merciful Father as prodigal sons. Rejoice always for the grace of being children of God and bring this joy to the world.

—*General Audience, June 4, 2014*

Why do I like being with young people? Because you have the promise of hope in your heart. You are bearers of hope. It is true that you live in the present, but you are looking towards the future ... You are architects of the future, artisans of the future ... Why? Mainly because inside you, you have three desires: [First], the desire for beauty. You like beauty and when you make music, produce theatre, and paint—beautiful things—you are looking for beauty, you are searching for beauty. Second, you are prophets of goodness. You like goodness and being good. And this goodness is contagious, it helps everyone else. And third, you thirst for the truth. Seek the truth. "But, Father, I possess the truth!" You are wrong because we cannot possess truth ...We must encounter it. It is an encounter with the truth that is God that we must search for.

These three desires that you have in your heart you must carry forward to the future [in order to] make the future beautiful with goodness and truth. Have you understood? This is a challenge; it is your challenge. But if you are lazy, if you are sad ...well, that beauty will not be beauty, that goodness will not be goodness, and that truth will be something else...Think about this carefully: Set your sights on a high ideal, the ideal of making a world of goodness, beauty, and truth. You can do this, you have the power to do it. If you do not do it, it is because of laziness. I wanted to tell you this; this is what I wanted to say to you.

I wanted to tell you this and to say to you: Have courage, go forward, and make noise. Where there are young people there should be noise. Then things settle down, but the dream of a young person is to make noise forever. Go ahead! In life there will always be people who suggest that you slow down, blocking your path. Please go against the current. Be courageous boys and girls. Go against the current...Go against the tide of this civilization that is harming itself. Do you understand this? Go against the current—and this means making noise. Go ahead, but with the values of beauty, goodness, and truth.

—*Address to the Young People of Piacenza-Bobbio,*
August 28, 2013

Courage! This is a virtue and an attribute of young people. The world needs courageous—not fearful—young people. It needs young people on the move, not standing still; there is no progress if the young stand still! Young people who are always motivated, not young people who are retired! It's sad to see a retired young person. No, a young person should go forward on this road of courage. Go forward! This will be your victory. Your job is to help change this world, to make it so much better...

—Address to the Agesci Scouts, August 10, 2014

Will the future be better or worse? I don't have a wizard's crystal ball to tell the future. But I will tell you one thing: Do you know where the future is? It is in your heart. It is in your mind and in your hands. If you feel good, if you think hard, and if you carry forward these good thoughts and good feelings in your hands, the future will be better. The future is for young people. But please note, [we need] young people with two qualities: young people with wings and young people with roots. Young people with wings to fly, dream, and create, and with roots to receive the wisdom that the elderly give. Therefore the future is in your hands—if you have wings and roots. Take the courage to have wings, to dream of good things, to dream of a better world, to protest wars. On the other hand, to respect the wisdom that you have received from those who are older than you, your parents, your grandparents, the elderly of your country. The future is in your hands. Take the opportunity to make it better.

—Video conference with students of the Scholas Social Network
September 4, 2014

To know God is strength. In other words, to know God, to draw closer to Jesus, is hope and strength. And that is what we need from young people today. We need young people full of hope and strength. We don't want "namby-pambies," young people who are just there, lukewarm, unable to say either yes or no. We don't want young people who tire quickly and who are always weary, with bored faces. We want young people who are strong. We want young people full of hope and strength. Why? Because they know Jesus. Because they know God. Because they have a heart that is free. A heart that is free, please repeat this.

[The young people repeat the words, "A heart that is free."]

Solidarity, work, hope, effort. To know Jesus. To know God, my strength. Can a young person who lives this way have a bored look on his face?

["No!"]

A sad heart?

["No!"]

This then is the path! But it is a path that requires sacrifice; it requires going against the tide.

So make a ruckus! But also help in cleaning it up. Two things: make a ruckus, but do a good job of it! A ruckus that brings us freedom of heart, a ruckus that brings solidarity, a ruckus that brings us hope, a ruckus that comes from knowing Jesus and realizing that God, once I know him, is my strength. That is the kind of ruckus that you should make.

Meeting with Young People, Asunción, Paraguay,
July 12, 2015

Dear young people, the most precious good that we can have in this life is our relationship with God. Are you convinced of this? Are you aware of the inestimable value that you have in God's eyes? Do you know that you are loved and accepted by him, unconditionally, as you are? Devoting time to prayer and the reading of scripture, especially the Gospels, you will come to know him, and yourselves, ever better. Today too, Jesus' counsels can illumine your feelings and your decisions. You are enthusiastic and generous, pursuing high ideals, searching for truth and beauty. I encourage you to maintain an alert and critical spirit in the face of every compromise that runs contrary to the gospel message.

—*Prayer Vigil with Young People, Bangui, Central African Republic*
November 29, 2015

To Students

Dear young people, if I were to ask you now, why do you go to school, what would your answer be? There would probably be a whole range of replies... Yet I think that they could all be summed up by saying that school is one of the educational environments in which we develop through learning how to live, how to become grown-up, mature men and women who can travel, who can follow the road of life. How does school help you to grow? It does so not only by helping you develop your intelligence but also by contributing to the integral formation of all the aspects of your personality.

According to what Saint Ignatius teaches us, the main [point of] school is to learn to be magnanimous. Magnanimity: this virtue of the great and the small, which always makes us look at the horizon. What does being magnanimous mean? It means having a great heart, having greatness of mind; it means having high ideals, the wish to do great things to respond to what God asks of us. Hence also, for this very reason, to do well the routine things of every day and all the daily actions, the tasks, the meetings with people; to do the little everyday things with a great heart open to God and to others. It is therefore important to foster human formation with a view to magnanimity. School broadens not only your intellectual dimension but also your human one. And I think that Jesuit schools take special care to develop human virtues: loyalty, respect, faithfulness, and dedication.

I would like to reflect on two fundamental values: freedom and service. First of all, be free people! What do I mean by this? One might think that freedom means doing everything one likes, or seeking out extreme experiences so that one can feel elation and overcome boredom. This is not freedom. Freedom means being able to think about what we do, being able to assess what is good and what is bad. These are the types of conduct that lead to development. Freedom means always opting for the good. Let us be free for goodness. And in this do not be afraid to go against the tide, even if it is not easy! Always being free to choose goodness is demanding, but it will make you into people with backbone who can face life, people with courage and patience.

The second value is service. In your schools you take part in various activities that accustom you to not retreat into yourselves or into your own small world but rather to be open to others, especially the poorest and neediest, to work hard to improve the world in which we live. Be men and women with others and for others true champions at the service of others.

In order to be magnanimous with inner freedom and a spirit of service, spiritual formation is necessary. Dear young people, love Jesus Christ more and more! Our life is a response to his call and you will be happy and will build your life well if you can answer this call. May you feel the Lord's presence in your life. He is close to each one of you as a companion, as a friend who knows how to help and understand you, who encourages you in difficult times and never abandons you. In prayer, in conversation with him, and in reading the Bible you will discover that he is truly close. You will also learn to read God's signs in your life. He always speaks to us, through the events of our times and of our daily life; it is up to us to listen to him.

—Address to the students of the Jesuit schools of Italy and Albania,
June 7, 2013

WHY ARE WE STUDYING?

I have a question for you, dear students who are here … You are the present and future, the ones who must stir things up. You are the seeds of your society's future growth. Do you realize that this time of study is not only a right, but also a privilege? How many of your friends, known or unknown, would like to have a place in this house but, for various reasons, do not? To what extent do our studies help us and bring us to feel solidarity with them? Ask yourselves these questions, dear students.

Educational communities play a fundamental role, an essential role, in the enrichment of civic and cultural life. Be careful! It is not enough to analyze and describe reality: we need to create environments, spaces for searching, for engaging in conversations that can lead to alternatives to current problems, especially today. We need to move to the concrete...It is urgent today that you, and I, and everyone continue reflecting on and talking about our current situation. I use the term "urgent" because there is a pressing need for us to think about the culture, the kind of culture, that we want not only for ourselves but for our children and our grandchildren. We have received this earth as an inheritance, as a gift, in trust. We would do well to ask ourselves: What kind of world do we want to leave behind? What meaning or direction do we want to give to our lives? Why have we been put here? What is the purpose of our work and all our efforts? (cf. *Laudato Si'*, 160). Why are we studying?

Personal initiatives are always necessary and good. But we are asked to go one step further, to start viewing reality in an organic and un-fragmented way, to ask about where we stand in relation to others, inasmuch as "everything is interconnected" (*Laudato Si'*, 138). There is no right to exclusion.

As a university, as educational institutions, as teachers and students, we are faced with a challenge posed by life itself, a challenge that involves answering these two questions: What does this world need us for? Where is your brother?

May the Holy Spirit inspire and accompany us, for he has summoned us, invited us, given us the opportunity and the duty to offer the best of ourselves. He is the same Spirit who on the first day of creation moved over the waters, ready to transform them, ready to bestow life. He is the same Spirit who gave the disciples the power of Pentecost. The Spirit does not abandon us. He becomes one with us, so that we can encounter paths of new life. May he, the Spirit, always be our companion and our teacher along the way.

> —*Meeting with educators, Pontifical Catholic University of Ecuador, Quito, July 7, 2015*

NEVER STOP DREAMING

A Latin American writer once said that we all have two eyes: one of flesh and another of glass. With the eye of flesh, we see what is in front of us. With the eye of glass, we see what we dream of. Beautiful, isn't it?

In the daily reality of life, there has to be room for dreaming. A young person incapable of dreaming is cut off, self-enclosed. Everyone sometimes dreams of things which are never going to happen. But dream them anyway, desire them, seek new horizons, be open to great things.

Dream that with you the world can be different. Dream that if you give your best, you are going to help make this world a different place. Don't forget to dream! If you get carried away and dream too much, life will cut you short. It makes no difference; dream anyway, and share your dreams. Talk about the great things you wish for, because the greater your ability to dream—even if life cuts you short halfway—the farther you will have gone. So, first of all, dream!

> —*Address to students, Fr. Félix Varela Cultural Center, Havana, Cuba, September 20, 2015*

I am very happy to be with you today, together with this big family that surrounds you. I see your teachers, your parents, and your family members. Thank you for letting me come, and I ask pardon from your teachers for "stealing" a few minutes of their class time. I know that you don't mind that!

They tell me that one of the nice things about this school, about your work, is that some students come from other places, and many from other countries. That is nice—even though I know that it is not easy to have to move and find a new home, to meet new neighbors and new friends. It is not easy, but you have to start. At the beginning it can be pretty hard. Often you have to learn a new language, adjust to a new culture, even a new climate. There is so much to learn! And it's not just homework, but so other many things too.

The good thing is that we also make new friends. This is very important, the new friends we make. We meet people who open doors for us, who are kind to us. They offer us friendship and understanding, and they try to help us not feel like strangers, foreigners. People work hard to help us feel at home. Even if we sometimes think back on where we came from, we meet good people who help us feel at home. How nice it is to feel that our school, or the places where we gather, are a second home. This is not only important for you, but also for your families. School then ends up being one big family, a family where, together with our mothers and fathers, our grandparents, our teachers and friends, we learn to help one another, to share our good qualities, to give the best of ourselves, to work as a team— for that is very important—and to pursue our dreams.

Very near here is a very important street named after a man who did a lot for other people. I want to talk a little bit

about him. He was the Reverend Martin Luther King. One day he said, "I have a dream." His dream was that many children, many people, could have equal opportunities. His dream was that many children like you could get an education. He dreamed that many men and women, like yourselves, could lift their heads high in dignity and self-sufficiency. It is beautiful to have dreams and to be able to fight for our dreams. Don't ever forget this.

Today we want to keep dreaming. We celebrate all the opportunities that enable you, and us adults too, not to lose the hope of a better world with greater possibilities. So many of the people I have met are also dreaming with you, they are dreaming of this. That is why they are doing this work. They are involved in your lives to help you move ahead. All of us dream. Always. I know that one of the dreams of your parents and teachers...is that you can grow up and be happy. Here I see you smiling. Keep smiling and help bring joy to everyone you meet. It isn't always easy. Every home has its problems, difficult situations, sickness, but never stop dreaming so you can be happy...

Before going, I would like to give you some homework. May I? It is just a little request, but a very important one. Please don't forget to pray for me, so that I can share with many people the joy of Jesus. And let us also pray that many other people can share joy like the joy you feel whenever you feel supported, helped, and counseled, even when there are problems. Even then, we still feel peace in our hearts, because Jesus never abandons us.

—Meeting with children and immigrant families,
Our Lady, Queen of Angels School, Harlem, New York, September 25, 2015

THINK, FEEL, AND DO!

Leandro Santos [in his words welcoming me here] asked questions about information and technology. Today, with so many kinds of media, we are informed, even over-informed. Is this a bad thing? No. It is good and useful, but we do run the risk of information overload. We have plenty of information, but maybe we don't know what to do with it all. We risk becoming "museums," storing up all sorts of things but not knowing what to do with them. We don't need young people who are storehouses, but young people who are wise.

You might ask me: Father, how can I become wise? This is another challenge, the challenge of love. What is the most important lesson that you have to learn in college? What is the most important lesson that you have to learn in life? It is learning how to love. This is the challenge that life sets before you today. Learning how to love—not just how to accumulate information. There comes a time when you don't know what to do with it all. It's a storehouse. Unless, through love, all this information can bear fruit.

For this to happen, the Gospel proposes to us a serene and tranquil thing to do. It is to use the three languages: the language of the mind, the language of the heart, and the language of the hands. All three together, harmoniously: what you think, what you feel, and what you do. Your information goes down to the heart, moves it, and gets translated into action. And all this in a harmonious way: I think what I feel and what I do, I feel what I think and what I do,

and I do what I think and what I feel. The three languages. Are you ready to repeat these three languages? Thinking, feeling, and acting. Say those words back to me. And all of this harmoniously.

True love is both loving and letting oneself be loved. It is harder to let ourselves be loved than it is to love. That is why it is so hard to achieve the perfect love of God, because while we can love him, the important thing is to let ourselves be loved by him. True love is being open to that love which was there first and catches us by surprise. If all you have is information, you are closed to surprises. Love makes you open to surprises. Love is always a surprise, because it starts with a dialogue between two persons: the one who loves and the one who is loved. We say that God is the God of surprises, because he always loved us first and he waits to take us by surprise. God surprises us. Let's allow ourselves to be surprised by God. Let's not have the psychology of a computer, thinking that we know everything. What do I mean? Think for a moment: the computer has all the answers—never a surprise. In the challenge of love, God shows up with surprises.

So let yourselves be surprised by God! Don't be afraid of surprises, afraid that they will shake you up. They make us insecure, but they get us moving. True love drives you to be unstinting with life, even at the risk of coming up empty-handed. Think of Saint Francis: he left everything, he died with empty hands, but with a full heart.

Do you agree? Not young people who are "museums" or "storehouses," but young people who are wise. To be wise, use the three languages well: think, feel, and act. And

to be wise, let yourselves be surprised by God's love, then go out and be unstinting with life!

—Meeting with young people at the sports field of Santo Tomás University, Manila, the Philippines, January 18, 2015

WHAT PATH SHOULD I CHOOSE?

What Marina said really struck me: about the conflict she felt in her life. What to do in this situation? Take up the path of consecrated life, religious life, or study to be better able to help others?

This is only an apparent conflict, because when the Lord calls, he always does so for the good of others, whether it is through the religious life, the consecrated life, or as a lay person, as the father or mother of a family. The goal is the same: to worship God and to do good to others. What should Marina do, and the many others of you who are asking the same question? I once asked it myself: What path should I choose? But you do not have to choose any path! The Lord must choose it! Jesus has chosen it! You have to listen to him and ask: "Lord, what should I do?"

This is the prayer that a young person should make: "Lord, what do you want from me?" With prayer and the advice of some good friends—laity, priests, religious sisters, bishops, popes (even the pope can offer some good advice!)—you can find the path that the Lord wants for you.

Let us pray together! Lord, what do you want from my life? Three times. Let us pray!

Then let us return to Marina. Marina proposed two questions...not so much two questions as two reflections and a question about happiness. She told us something very true: you cannot purchase happiness. Whenever you buy happiness, you soon realize that it has vanished: The happiness you buy does not last. Only the happiness of love is the kind that lasts.

The path of love is simple: love God and love your neighbor, your brother or sister, the one at your side who needs love and so many other things. "But Father, how do I know that I love God?" Only if you love your neighbor, if you do not hate your neighbor and do not harbor hatred in your heart, do you love God. This is the sure proof.

None of us knows what life will bring us. And you, dear young friends, are asking: "What is in store for me?" We are capable of doing bad things, very bad things, but please, do not despair: the Father is always there waiting for us! Come back! Come back! This is the word: Come back! Come back home because the Father is waiting for me. And if I am a great sinner, he will celebrate the more. To hear this is something beautiful. It is something that brings me great happiness, to know that God never tires of forgiving; he never tires of waiting for us.

—*Shrine of Solmoe, Republic of Korea, Sixth Asian Youth Day, August 15, 2014*

Conversations

THE ART OF WALKING...

A boy: I am a boy who seeks to believe. I am searching...search-ing, yes, to be faithful. However I have difficulties. Sometimes doubts come to me...I wanted to ask you for a few words to help me in my growth and to support all the other young people like me.

Pope Francis: Walking is an art; if we are always in a hurry, we tire and cannot reach our destination, the destination of our journey. Yet if we stop and do not move, we also fail to reach our destination. Walking is precisely the art of look-ing to the horizon, thinking about where I want to go, and also coping with the weariness that comes from walking. Moreover, the way often involves hard going. It is not easy. "I want to stay faithful to this journey, but it is not easy..." Yet always keep this in your thoughts: do not be afraid of failure, do not be afraid of falling. In the art of walking it is not falling that matters, but not "staying fallen." Get up quickly, immediately, and continue to go on...But also: it is terrible to walk alone, terrible and tedious. Walking in community, with friends, with those who love us: this helps us; it helps us to arrive precisely at the destination that is our goal.

A boy: *How did you get through it, when you decided to become a parish priest, to become a Jesuit? How did you do it? Wasn't it difficult for you to abandon or leave your family and friends?*

Pope Francis: You know, it is always difficult. Always. It was hard for me. It is far from easy. There are beautiful moments, and Jesus helps you, he gives you a little joy. All the same there are difficult moments when you feel alone, when you feel dry, without any interior joy. There are clouded moments of interior darkness. There are hardships. But it is so beautiful to follow Jesus, to walk in the footsteps of Jesus, that you can find balance and move forward. And then come even more wonderful moments. But no one must think that there will not be difficult moments in life. I would now like to ask a question myself. How do you think you can move forward with the hardships? It isn't easy, but we must go ahead with strength and with trust in the Lord. With the Lord everything is possible.

—*With the students of the Jesuit schools of Italy and Albania, June 7, 2013*

WITH THE POOR JESUS

A young man: *Father, we have learned to coexist with many different kinds of poverty: material poverty, spiritual poverty, the injuries of political events or of alcoholism. How can we young people live with this poverty? How should we behave?*

Pope Francis: First of all, I would like to say one thing to all you young people: do not let yourselves be robbed of hope! Please, do not let yourselves be robbed of it! And who robs you of hope? The spirit of the world, wealth, the spirit of vanity, arrogance, pride. All these things steal hope from you. Where do I find hope? In the poor Jesus, Jesus who made himself poor for us. And you mentioned poverty. Poverty demands that we sow hope. It requires me to have greater hope, too...Poverty is the flesh of the poor Jesus in this hungry child, in the sick person, in these unjust social structures. Go, look over there at the flesh of Jesus. But do not let yourselves be robbed of hope by well-being, by the spirit of well-being which, in the end brings you to become a nothing in life! The young must be willing to risk themselves for high ideals: this is my advice. But where do I find hope? In the flesh of the suffering Jesus and in true poverty. There is a connection between the two.

A young woman: I was wondering: Why you have renounced the riches of a pope, like a luxurious apartment and a large car? Instead you have opted for a small apartment close by, and you even took the bus for bishops. Why ever did you give up riches?

Pope Francis: Well, I believe it is not only a matter of wealth. For me it is a question of personality: that is what it is. I need to live with people, and were I to live alone, perhaps a little isolated, it wouldn't be good for me...And then I believe, yes: the times speak to us of such great poverty throughout the world, and this is a scandal. The poverty of the world is a scandal. In a world where there is such great wealth, so many resources for giving food to everyone, it is impossible to understand how there could be so many hungry children, so many children without education, so many poor people! Poverty today is a cry. We must all think about whether we can become a little poorer. This is something we must all do. How I can become a little poorer to be more like Jesus, who was the poor Teacher? This is the thing. But it is not a problem of my personal virtue, it is only that I cannot live alone . . .

—*With the students of the Jesuit schools of Italy and Albania, June 7, 2013*

TRUE PEACE, FALSE PEACE

Thank you very much for your questions. There are two words, at the beginning of the questions [you asked me], that struck me, and they are words that one lives in everyday life, both in society and in the family. The words are "tension" and "conflict." . . . Let us think, what would a society, a family, a group of friends be like without tension and conflict? Do you know what it would be? A cemetery. Because only in dead things are there no tensions and no conflicts. Where there is life, there is tension and there is conflict. That is why it is necessary to look for what the real tensions are in my life, how they arise, because it is tension that says I am alive . . . Tension makes one grow; it develops courage. A young person must have the virtue of courage. A youth without courage is a young person who is "watered down," an aged youth. Sometimes I have wanted to say to young people: "Please, do not retire!"—because there are young people who retire at the age of twenty.

Everything is secure in life, everything is calm, there is no "tension."

It is clear that there is tension in the family. How does one resolve tension? With dialogue. When there is dialogue in a family, when there is the capacity to spontaneously speak one's mind, tensions can be resolved very well...

The Pelé fan [a Brazilian girl] asked this question: What has been the greatest challenge or difficulty that Pope Francis has faced in his mission as a religious? I would say: always seeking peace in the Lord, that peace which Jesus alone can give you. At work, in tasks, the challenge is to find that peace which means that the Lord accompanies you, that the Lord is close. And there is also another challenge: to know how to distinguish the peace of Jesus from another kind of peace, one that is not of Jesus. Do you understand?

This is something that you must learn well. Ask the Lord for the grace to know how to discern true peace from false peace. To discern. This is a challenge. And true peace always comes from Jesus. Sometimes it comes "wrapped" in a cross. But it is Jesus who gives you peace in that trial. It does not always come as a cross, but true peace always comes from Jesus. Instead, the other kind of peace, the superficial kind, the peace that makes you happy and somewhat content but is superficial, that peace comes from the enemy, from the devil, and it makes you happy: "I'm content, I'm not worried about this, I'm at peace..." But inside, it's fake!

Here it is necessary to ask for this grace, to know how to distinguish, to know how to recognize which is the peace of Jesus and which is the peace that comes from the enemy, which destroys you. The enemy always destroys: he makes you believe that this is the way and then, in the end, he leaves you on your own. Because remember this: the devil is a poor payer, he never pays well! He always cheats, he's a swindler! He shows you things dressed up, so you believe a thing is good, that it will give you peace; you go there and in the end you don't find happiness.

To always seek the peace of Jesus: this is a challenge, a challenge that I have had, that I have, and that all of you have. What is the sign of Jesus' peace? How do I know that this peace is given by Jesus? The sign is joy, profound joy. The devil never gives you joy. He gives you a little entertainment, a "pantomime," he makes you happy for a moment, but he never gives you that joy. It is a joy Jesus alone can give, by giving you the Holy Spirit. The challenge for all of us—for me too—is always to seek the peace of Jesus, even in dark times, but the peace of Jesus. And to know how to distinguish it from that other, false kind of peace, which in the end is dishonest: it ends badly and does not reward you properly. Jesus is a good payer, he pays well: he pays very well!

—*Address to the Eucharistic Youth Movement (MEG), August 7, 2015*

ANSWERS TO YOUNG PEOPLE'S QUESTIONS

Thank you for having accepted our request [to meet with you], but why did you do so?

Pope Francis: When I hear that a young man or woman is restless, I feel that it is my duty to serve these young people, to address this restlessness, because it is like a seed, and later it will go on to bear fruit. And, in this moment I feel that with you I am helping you deal with that which is most precious, in this moment, which is your restlessness.

A boy: Everyone in the world seeks to be happy. But, we asked ourselves, are you happy? And, why?

Pope Francis: Absolutely, absolutely, I am happy. I'm happy because...I don't know why...maybe because I have a job, I am not unemployed, I have work, a job as a shepherd! I am happy because I found my path in life and walking this path makes me happy. And it is also a serene happiness, because at this age it is not the same happiness as that of a young person, there is a difference; there is a certain interior peace, a great peace, a happiness that also comes with age. And also with a journey that has always had problems. Even now there are problems, but this happiness doesn't go away with the problems, no. It sees the problems, suffers them, and then moves on. It does something to resolve them and moves ahead. But in the depths of the heart, there is this peace and this happiness. It is a grace of God, for me, truly. It is a grace. I don't deserve it at all.

A girl: I don't believe in God, but your actions and your ideals inspire me. Perhaps you have a message for all of us, for the young Christians, for people who don't believe or have other beliefs or believe in a different way?

Pope Francis: For me, one must seek, in a way of speaking, authenticity. And for me, authenticity is this: I am speaking with my brothers. We are all brothers. Believers, non-believers, or those of one religious confession or another, Jews, Muslims…we are all brothers. Humanity is at the center of history, and this for me is very important: humanity is at the center. In this moment of history, humanity has been thrown out of the center…and at the center is power, money. And we must work for people, for men and women, who are the image of God. Why young people? Because the young—and here I go back to what I said at the beginning—are the seed that will bear fruit along the path. But also in relation to that which I was saying now: in this world, where power and money are at the center, young people are chased away. Children are chased away; we don't want kids, we want fewer of them, small families. Children aren't wanted. The elderly are chased away. So many elderly people die by way of a hidden euthanasia, because they are not cared for and they die. And now young people are chased away…I believe that we must help young people so that they might take up the role in society that is needed in this difficult historical moment.

But do you have a specific, very concrete message for us, so that we—perhaps—might inspire other people as you do? Even people who don't believe?

You've said a very important word: "concrete." It is an extremely important word, because in the concreteness of life you move forward. With ideas alone, you don't move forward! This is very important. And, I believe that you young people must move forward with this concreteness in life...I believe that youth, in this moment, must be aware of the tempo and move ahead. Be courageous! This gives me hope.

A girl: Since I don't believe in God, I am unable to understand how you pray or why you pray. Can you explain how you pray?

Pope Francis: How I pray...Often I take the Bible, I read it a bit, then I leave it and I let myself be looked at by the Lord. That is the most common idea in my prayer. I allow myself to be looked at by him. And I feel—but it isn't sentimentalism—I feel deeply the things that the Lord tells me. Sometimes he doesn't speak...nothing, empty, empty, empty...but patiently I am there, and I pray this way...I am seated, I pray seated, because it hurts me to kneel, and sometimes I fall asleep in prayer...It is also a way of praying, as a son with the Father, and this is important. I feel like a son with the Father.

And why do I pray? I pray because I need to. This is something I feel, something that pushes me, as if God has called me to speak. And I pray for people, when I meet people who touch my heart because they are sick or have problems, or when I see problems like, for example, war...

I have my fears. What are you afraid of?

Look, in the Gospel, Jesus repeats often, "Do not be afraid! Do not be afraid!" So many times he says it. And, why?

Because he knows that fear is a normal thing. We are fearful of life, we are afraid before the challenges, we are afraid before God ... All of us are afraid, everyone. You should not be worried about being afraid. You must feel this but not be afraid, and then think, "Why am I scared?" And, before God and before yourself, seek to clarify the situation or ask for the help of another ...

Our last question, do you have a question for us?

The question I want to ask you is not original. I take it from the Gospel. But I think that after hearing it, maybe it will be the right one for you at this moment. Where is your treasure? This is the question. Where does your heart rest? On what treasure does your heart rest? Because there where your treasure is will be your life. The heart is attached to the treasure. There can be so many treasures: power, money, pride, ... or goodness, beauty, the will to do good ... Where is your treasure? This is the question I would like to ask you, but you will have to give the response yourselves, alone! In your home ...

—*Conversation with Belgian Youth, Vatican City, April 7, 2014*

ON NOT LOSING HOPE

A Kenyan boy: How can we realize that God is our Father? How can we see God's hand in the tragedies of life? How can we find God's peace?

Pope Francis: This sounds like the question of a theology professor! This question is asked by men and women the world over in one way or another. And they don't come up with an answer. There are some questions to which, no matter how hard we try, we never seem to find an answer. "How can I see the hand of God in one of life's tragedies?" There is only one answer: no, there is no answer. There is only a way: *to look to the Son of God.* God delivered his Son to save us all. God let himself get hurt. God let himself be destroyed on the cross. So when the moment comes when you don't understand, when you're in despair and the world is tumbling down all around you, *look to the cross!* There we see the failure of God; there we see the destruction of God. But there we also see a challenge to our faith: the challenge of hope. Because that story didn't end in failure. There was *the resurrection,* which made all things new.

I'll tell you a secret. In my pocket I always carry two things: a rosary, to pray, and something else which may seem a little odd ... What is it? It's the story of God's failure: it is a little Way of the Cross, the story of how Jesus suffered from the time he was condemned to death until his burial. With these two things, I try to do my best. And thanks to these two things I don't lose hope.

—*Meeting with Young People, Nairobi, Kenya, November 27, 2015*

MEETINGS
WITH YOUNG PEOPLE

Go Out into the Deep!

Meeting with the Young People of Sardinia
Largo Carlo Felice, Cagliari, September 22, 2013

Dear Young People of Sardinia,

Thank you for coming to this meeting in such large numbers! I am thinking of the Gospel, by the shores of the Sea of Galilee, where Simon, whom Jesus was later to call Peter, and his brother Andrew, together with James and John, also brothers, all of whom lived and worked as fishermen. Jesus was surrounded by the crowd of people who wanted to listen to his word. He saw those fishermen mending their nets beside their boats. He climbed into Simon's boat and asked him to put out a little from the shore. So it was that he spoke to the people as he sat in the boat; Jesus addressed the people from the boat. When he had finished, he told Simon to put out into the deep and let down his nets. This request was a "trial" for Simon—listen carefully to the word: a "trial," for he and the others had just come back from fishing all night with nothing to show for it. Simon was a sincere and practical man, and he immediately said to Jesus: "Master, we toiled all night and caught nothing."

This is the first point: *the experience of failure.* In your questions there was this experience: the sacrament of confirmation. What is this sacrament called? Confirmation... No! Its name has changed to the "sacrament of farewell." They do this and then they leave the Church. Is this true or not? This is an experience of failure. The sacrament of farewell, of goodbye, is an experience of failure, an experience that leaves emptiness and discourages us. Is this true or not?

["Yes!" the young people answer.]

Is it true or not?

["Yes!" they answer once again.]

In the face of this situation you are right to wonder: What can we do? Of course one thing is to let oneself be overcome by pessimism and distrust. Pessimistic Christians: how awful! You young people can't and mustn't be lacking in hope. Hope is part of your being. A young person without hope is not young but has aged prematurely! Hope is part of your youth! A young person without joy and without hope is upsetting: that person is not young. Let's return to the scene of the Gospel: Peter, in that critical moment, takes a risk. What could he have done? He could have given in to weariness and to discouragement, thinking that continuing would be pointless and that it was better to withdraw and go home. Instead, what does he do? With courage, he steps out of himself and decides to trust Jesus. He says: "Well, all right! At your word I will let down the nets." But notice! He does not say: with my strength, my calculations, my experience as an expert fisherman, but rather "at your word"—at the word of Jesus! And the result is an incredible catch, the nets are filled to the point that they almost tear.

This is the second point: *trusting Jesus, trusting Jesus.* And when I say this I want to be sincere and to tell you that I do not come here to sell you an illusion. I come here to say: there is a person who can keep you going, trust in him! It is Jesus! Trust in Jesus! And Jesus is not an illusion! Trust in Jesus. The Lord is always with us. He comes to the shores of the sea of our life, he draws near to us in our failures, our frailty, and our sins in order to transform them. Never stop trusting him; be willing, over and over again, as good athletes—some of you know this well from experience—to face the strain of training in order to achieve results! Difficulties must not frighten you; on the contrary, they should spur you to go beyond them. Hear Jesus' words as though they were addressed to you: put out into the deep and let down your nets, young people of Sardinia! Put out into the deep!

Be ever more docile to the Lord's word; it is he, it is his word, it is following him that brings to fruition your commitment to witnessing. When your efforts to reawaken faith in your friends seem to be in vain, like the nighttime efforts of the fishermen, remember that with Jesus everything changes. The word of the Lord has filled the nets, and the word of the Lord makes the missionary work of his disciples effective. Following Jesus is demanding, it means not being satisfied with small goals of little account but aiming high with courage!

It is not good to stop at "we caught nothing"; rather, go further, "put out into the deep and let down your nets" once again, and without tiring! Jesus repeats this to each one of you. And it is he who will give you the strength! There is the threat of complaining or of resignation. Let's leave these epithets to the followers of the "goddess of lamentation." And you, are you following the "goddess of lamentation"? Are you continuously wailing as in a funeral wake? No, young people can't do that! The "goddess of lamentation" is a deception: she makes you take the wrong road. When everything seems to be standing still and stagnant, when personal problems disturb us and social hardships go unaddressed and needs are unmet, it is not good to consider oneself vanquished. Jesus is the way: we must have him embark on our "boat" and put out into the deep with him! He is the Lord! He changes the prospect of life. Faith in Jesus leads to a hope that goes further, to a certainty based not on our qualities and skills alone, but on the word of God, on the invitation that comes from him. Without making too many human calculations and without worrying about checking whether the situation that surrounds us corresponds with our need for security. We need to put out into the deep, go out of ourselves: go out of our small world and open ourselves to God, open ourselves increasingly also to our brothers and sisters. Opening ourselves to God is opening ourselves to others. Let us take a few steps outside ourselves, little steps, but let us take them. Let us go out of yourselves toward God and toward others, opening our hearts to our brothers and sisters, to friendship, and to solidarity...

Have I gone on for too long?

[*"No!" the young people reply.*]

Let's stay united in prayer. And journey on in this life with Jesus: the saints did it.

Saints are like this: they are not born perfect, already holy! They become so because, like Simon Peter, they trust in the word of the Lord and "put out into the deep." Your land has contributed so many witnesses. They are ordinary people who, instead of complaining, "let down their nets for a catch." Imitate their example, entrust yourselves to their intercession, and always be men and women of hope! No complaining! No discouragement! Never be depressed, never seek to purchase comfort from death: none of it! Go forward with Jesus! He never fails, he never disappoints, he is loyal!

By the Witness of Our Lives

Meeting with the Young People of Umbria, Assisi
October 4, 2013

Dear young people of Umbria,

Good evening! Thank you for coming, thank you for this celebration! And thank you for your questions.

Dear friends, the Gospel does not only concern religion. It concerns humanity, the whole of humanity; it concerns the world, society, and human civilization. The Gospel is God's message of salvation for humanity. When we say "message of salvation," this is not simply a way of speaking, these are not mere words or empty words like so many today. Humanity truly needs to be saved! We see it every day when we flip through newspapers or watch the news on television; but we also see it around us, in people, in situations; and we see it in ourselves! Each one of us needs to be saved! We cannot do it alone! We need to be saved! Saved from what? From evil. Evil is at work, it does its job. However, evil is not invincible and a Christian does not give up when confronted by evil. And you young people, do you want to give up in the face of evil, injustice and difficulty? Do you want to or not?

[*The young people reply, "No!"*]

Ah, good. I like this. Our secret is that God is greater than evil: this is true! God is greater than evil. God is infinite love, boundless mercy, and that love has conquered evil at its root through the death and resurrection of Christ. This is the Gospel, the Good News: God's love has won! Christ died on the cross for our sins and rose again. With him we can fight evil and conquer every day. Do we believe this or not?

[*The young people reply, "Yes!"*]

But that "yes" has to become part of life! If I believe that Jesus has conquered evil and saved me, I must follow along the path of Jesus for my whole life.

The Gospel, then, this message of salvation, has two destinations that are connected: the first, to awaken faith, and this is evangelization; the second, to transform the world according to God's plan, and this is the Christian animation of society. But these are not two separate things, they form one mission: to carry the Gospel by the witness of our lives in order to transform the world! This is the way: to bring the Gospel by the witness of our lives.

Let us look to Saint Francis: he did both of these things, through the power of the one Gospel. Francis made faith grow and he renewed the Church, and at the same time he renewed society, he made it more fraternal, but he always did it with the Gospel and by his witness. Do you know what Francis once said to his brothers? He said: "Always preach the Gospel, and if necessary, use words!" But how? Is it possible to preach the Gospel without words? Yes! By your witness! First comes witness, then come words!

Christ Knocks on the Door of Your Heart

Meeting with Asian Youth
on the Occasion of the Sixth Asian Youth Day
Shrine of Solmoe, Republic of Korea, August 15, 2014

Dear Young Friends,

This afternoon I would like to reflect with you on part of the theme of this Sixth Asian Youth Day: "The Glory of the Martyrs Shines on You." Just as the Lord made his glory shine forth in the heroic witness of the martyrs, so too he wants to make his glory shine in your lives, and through you, to light up the life of this vast continent. Today Christ is knocking at the door of your heart, of my heart. He calls you and me to rise, to be wide awake and alert, and to see the things in life that really matter. What is more, he is asking you and me to go out on the highways and byways of this world, knocking on the doors of other people's hearts, inviting them to welcome him into their lives.

This great gathering of Asian young people also allows us to see something of what the Church herself is meant to be in God's eternal plan. Together with young people everywhere, you want to help build a world where we all live together in peace and friendship, overcoming barriers, healing divisions, rejecting violence and prejudice. And this is exactly what God wants for us. The Church is meant to be a seed of unity for the whole human family. In Christ, all nations and peoples are called to a unity which does not destroy diversity but acknowledges, reconciles, and enriches it.

How distant the spirit of the world seems from that magnificent vision and plan! How often the seeds of goodness and hope which we try to sow seem to be choked by weeds of selfishness, hostility, and injustice, not only all around us, but also in our own hearts. We are troubled by the growing gap in our societies between rich and poor. We see signs of an idolatry of wealth, power, and pleasure which come at a high cost to human lives. Closer to home, so many of our own friends and contemporaries, even in the midst of immense material prosperity, are suffering from spiritual poverty, loneliness, and quiet despair. God seems to be removed from the picture. It is almost as though a spiritual desert is beginning to spread throughout our world. It affects the young too, robbing them of hope and even, in all too many cases, of life itself.

Yet this is the world into which you are called to go forth and bear witness to the Gospel of hope, the Gospel of Jesus Christ, and the promise of his kingdom . . . In the parables, Jesus tells us that the kingdom comes into the world quietly, growing silently yet surely wherever it is welcomed by hearts open to its message of hope and salvation. The Gospel teaches us that the Spirit of Jesus can bring new life to every human heart and can transform every situation, even the most apparently hopeless. Jesus can transform all situations! This is the message which you are called to share with your contemporaries: at school, in the workplace, in your families, your universities, and your communities. Because Jesus rose from the dead, we know that he has "the words of eternal life" (Jn 6:68), that his word has the power to touch every heart, to conquer evil with good, and to change and redeem the world.

Dear young friends, in this generation the Lord is counting on you! He is counting on you! He entered your hearts on the day of your baptism; he gave you his Spirit on the day of your confirmation; and he strengthens you constantly by his presence in the Eucharist, so that you can be his witnesses before the world. Are you ready to say "yes"?

["*Yes!*"]

Are you ready?

["*Yes!*"]

Thank you!

Wake Up!

Closing Mass for the Sixth Asian Youth Day
Haemi Castle, Republic of Korea, August 17, 2014

Dear Young Friends,

The glory of the martyrs shines upon you! These words—a part of the theme of the Sixth Asian Youth Day—console and strengthen us all. Young people of Asia: you are the heirs of a great testimony, a precious witness to Christ. He is the light of the world; he is the light of our lives! The martyrs of Korea—and innumerable others throughout Asia—handed over their bodies to their persecutors; to us they have handed on a perennial witness that the light of Christ's truth dispels all darkness, and the love of Christ is gloriously triumphant. With the certainty of his victory over death, and our participation in it, we can face the challenge of Christian discipleship today, in our own circumstances and time.

The words which we have just reflected upon are a consolation. The other part of this day's theme—*Asian Youth! Wake up!*—speaks to you of a duty, a responsibility. Let us consider for a moment each of these words.

First, the word *"Asian."* You have gathered here in Korea from all parts of Asia. Each of you has a unique place and context where you are called to reflect God's love. The Asian continent, imbued with rich philosophical and religious traditions, remains a great frontier for your testimony to Christ, "the way, and the truth and the life" (Jn 14:6). As young people not only *in* Asia, but also as sons and daughters *of* this great continent, you have a right and a duty to take full part in the life of your societies. Do not be afraid to bring the wisdom of faith to every aspect of social life!

As Asians too, you see and love, from within, all that is beautiful, noble, and true in your cultures and traditions. And, as Christians, you also know that the Gospel has the power to purify, elevate, and perfect this heritage. Through the presence of the Holy Spirit given you in baptism and sealed within you at confirmation, and in union with your pastors, you can appreciate the many positive values of the diverse Asian cultures. You are also able to discern what is incompatible with your Catholic faith, what is contrary to the life of grace bestowed in baptism, and what aspects of contemporary culture are sinful, corrupt, and lead to death.

Returning to the theme of this day, let us reflect on a second word: *"Youth."* You and your friends are filled with the optimism, energy, and good will which are so characteristic of this period of life. Let Christ turn your natural optimism into Christian hope, your energy into moral virtue, your good will into genuine self-sacrificing love! This is the path you are called to take. This is the path to overcoming all that threatens hope, virtue, and love in your lives and in your culture. In this way your youth will be a gift to Jesus and to the world.

As young Christians, whether you are workers or students, whether you have already begun a career or have answered the call to marriage, religious life, or the priesthood, you are not only a part of the *future* of the Church; you are also a necessary and beloved part of the Church's *present*! You are the Church's present! Keep close to one another, draw ever closer to God, and with your bishops and priests spend these years building a holier, more missionary, and humble Church—a holier, more missionary and humble Church—a Church that loves and worships God by seeking to serve the poor, the lonely, the infirm and the marginalized.

In your Christian lives, you will find many occasions that will tempt you, like the disciples in today's Gospel, to push away the stranger, the needy, the poor, and the broken-hearted. It is these people especially who repeat the cry of the woman of the Gospel: "Lord, help me!" The Canaanite woman's plea is the cry of everyone who searches for love, acceptance, and friendship with Christ. It is the cry of so many people in our anonymous cities, the cry of so many of your own contemporaries, and the cry of all those martyrs who even today suffer persecution and death for the name of Jesus: "Lord, help me!" It is often a cry that rises from our own hearts as well: "Lord, help me!" Let us respond, not like those who push away people who make demands on us, as if serving the needy gets in the way of our being close to the Lord. No! We are to be like Christ, who responds to every plea for his help with love, mercy, and compassion.

Finally, the third part of this Day's theme—*"Wake up!"*—This word speaks of a responsibility which the Lord gives you. It is the duty to be vigilant, not to allow the pressures, the temptations, and the sins of ourselves or others to dull our sensitivity to the beauty of holiness, to the joy of the Gospel. Today's responsorial psalm invites us constantly to "be glad and sing for joy." No one who sleeps can sing, dance, or rejoice. I don't like to see young people who are sleeping. No! Wake up! Go! Go forward! Dear young people, "God, our God, has blessed us!" (Ps 67:6); from him we have "received mercy" (Rom 11:30). Assured of God's love, go out to the world so that, "by the mercy shown to you," they— your friends, co-workers, neighbors, fellow citizens, everyone on this great continent—"may now receive the mercy of God" (cf. Rom 11:31). It is by his mercy that we are saved.

Learning to Weep

Meeting with Young People
Sports Field of Santo Tomás University,
Manila, the Philippines, January 18, 2015

IMPROMPTU SPEECH OF THE HOLY FATHER

Dear Young Friends,

In a special way, I thank the young people who have offered words of welcome to me: Jun, Leandro, and Rikki. Thank you very much.

And the small...the small representation of women. Too small! Women have much to say to us in today's society. Sometimes we are too "machista"; we don't make room for women. Women are able to see things differently than men. Women can ask questions that we men just don't get. Pay attention. She [Jun's friend Glyzelle] today asked the one question that doesn't have an answer. And she couldn't say it in words. She had to say it with tears.

I thank you, Jun, for being so brave in talking about your experience. As I just said, your question, deep down, is almost unanswerable. Only when we are able to weep

47

over the things that you experienced can we understand
and give some kind of response. The great question for
everybody is: "Why do children suffer?" Why do children
suffer? Only when our hearts can ask this question and
weep can we begin to understand. There is a worldly compassion which is completely useless. (You said something
about this.) A compassion which, at most, makes us reach
into our pocket and take out a coin. If Christ had had that
kind of compassion, he would have passed by, cured three
or four people, and then returned to the Father. Only when
Christ wept, and he was capable of weeping, did he understand our troubles.

Dear young men and women, our world today needs
weeping. The marginalized weep, those who are neglected
weep, the scorned weep, but those of us who have rela-
tively comfortable life, we don't know how to weep. Certain realities of life are seen only with eyes that are
cleansed by tears. I invite each one of you to ask: Can I
weep? Can I weep when I see a child who is hungry, on
drugs and on the street, homeless, abandoned, mistreated,
or exploited as a slave by society? Or is my weeping the
self-centered whining of those who weep because they
want to have something else? This is the first thing I would
like to say to you. Let's learn to weep, the way [Glyzelle]
taught us today. Let's not forget this witness. She asked the
big question—why do children suffer?—by weeping; and
the big answer that we can give, all of us, is to learn how to
weep.

In the Gospel, Jesus wept. He wept for his dead friend.
He wept in his heart for the family that had lost its daugh-

ter. He wept in his heart when he saw the poor widowed mother who was burying her son. He was moved and he wept in his heart when he saw the crowds like sheep without a shepherd. If you don't learn how to weep, you are not a good Christian. And this is a challenge. Jun and his friend who spoke today posed this challenge. When they ask us: Why do children suffer? Why does this or that tragedy occur in life? Let us respond either by silence or with a word born of tears. Be brave. Don't be afraid to cry!

PREPARED SPEECH OF THE HOLY FATHER

Dear Young Friends,

It is a joy for me to be with you this morning. I greet each of you from the heart, and I thank all those who made this meeting possible. During my visit to the Philippines, I wanted in a particular way to meet with young people, to listen to you and to talk with you. I want to express the love and the hopes of the Church for you. And I want to encourage you, as Christian citizens of this country, to offer yourselves passionately and honestly to the great work of renewing your society and helping to build a better world.

Today I would like to suggest three key areas where you have a significant contribution to make to the life of your country. The first of these is *the challenge of integrity*. The word "challenge" can be understood in two ways. First, it can be understood negatively, as a temptation to act against your moral convictions, what you know to be true, good, and right. Our integrity can be challenged by selfish interest, greed, dishonesty, or the willingness to use other people.

But the word "challenge" can be also understood positively. It can be seen as invitation to courage, a summons to bear prophetic witness to what you believe and hold sacred. In this sense, the challenge of integrity is something that you have to face now, at this time in your lives. It is not something you can put off until you are older or have greater responsibilities. Even now you are challenged to act with honesty and fairness in your dealings with others, young and old alike. Do not avoid the challenge! One of the greatest challenges young people face is learning to love. To love means to take a risk: the risk of rejection, the risk of being taken advantage of or, worse, of taking advantage of another. Do not be afraid to love! But in love, too, maintain your integrity! Here too, be honest and fair!

A second key area where you are called to make a contribution is in showing *concern for the environment*. This is not only because this country, more than many others, is likely to be seriously affected by climate change. You are called to care for creation not only as responsible citizens but also as followers of Christ! Respect for the environment means more than simply using cleaner products or recycling what we use. These are important things, but they are not enough. We need to see, with the eyes of faith, the beauty of God's saving plan, the link between the natural environment and the dignity of the human person. Men and women are made in the image and likeness of God, and given dominion over creation (cf. Gen 1:26–28). As stewards of God's creation, we are called to make the earth a beautiful garden for the human family. When we destroy our forests, ravage our soil, and pollute our seas, we betray that noble calling.

A final area in which you can make a contribution is one dear to all of us. It is *care for the poor*. We are Christians. We are members of God's family. No matter how much or how little we have individually, each one of us is called to personally reach out and serve our brothers and sisters in need. There is always someone near us who is in need—materially, emotionally, spiritually. The greatest gift we can give is our friendship, our concern, our tenderness, our love for Jesus. To receive Jesus is to have everything; to give him is to give the greatest gift of all.

Many of you know what it is to be poor. But many of you have also experienced something of the blessedness that Jesus promised to "the poor in spirit" (cf. Mt 5:3). Here I would say a word of encouragement and gratitude to those of you who choose to follow our Lord in his poverty through a vocation to the priesthood and the religious life; by drawing on that poverty you will enrich many. But to all of you, especially those who can do more and give more, I ask: Please, do more! Please, give more! When you give of your time, your talents, and your resources to the many people who struggle and who live on the margins, you make a difference. It is a difference that is so desperately needed, and one for which you will be richly rewarded by the Lord. For, as he has said, "you will have treasure in heaven" (Mk 10:21).

Twenty years ago, in this very place, Saint John Paul II said that the world needs "a new kind of young person"—

one committed to the highest ideals and eager to build the civilization of love. Be those young persons! Never lose your idealism! Be joyful witnesses to God's love and the beautiful plan he has for us, for this country, and for the world in which we live. Please pray for me. God bless you all!

Love, Life, Friends

Meeting with Children and Young People
Piazza Vittorio, Turin, Italy, June 21, 2015

Thank you, because the questions you have asked are on the subject of the three words of John's Gospel that we heard: love, life, friends. These three words are intertwined in John's text, and one explains the other: one cannot speak of life in the Gospel—if we speak of real life—without speaking of love, and one cannot speak of love without this transformation from servants to friends. These three words are so important for life, but all three have a common root: the will to live. And I permit myself to recall here the words of Blessed Pier Giorgio Frassati, a young man like you: "Live, don't just get by!" Live!

You know that it is awful to see a youth "standing still," one who lives, but he lives—allow me the word—like a vegetable: he does things, but his life is not a life that moves, it stands still. You know that it makes me very sad at heart to see young people retire at twenty! Yes, they age quickly... And [this connects to] the question Chiara asked about love. The thing that keeps a young person from retiring is the desire to love, the desire to give what is most beautiful of man, and what is most beautiful of God, because the definition that John gives of God is "God is love." And when a young person loves, lives, grows, he does not retire. He grows, grows, grows and gives.

But what is love? "Is it a soap opera, Father? What we see on TV programs?" Some think that that is love. It is so good to speak of love, very beautiful, beautiful, beautiful things can be said. However, love has two axes on which it pivots, and if a person, a young person, doesn't have these two axes—these two dimensions of love—it's not love. First of all, *love is more in works than in words: love is concrete.* Love is concrete, it is more in deeds than in words. It's not love to just say: "I love you, I love all people." No. What do you do for love? Love gives itself. Consider that God began to speak of love when he engaged his people, when he chose his people, he made a covenant with his people, he saved his people, He forgave so many times—God has so much patience!—he made gestures of love, works of love.

And the second dimension, the second axis on which love pivots is that *love is always communicated,* that is, love listens and responds, *love is built in dialogue, in communion:* it is communicated. Love is neither deaf nor mute; it communicates. These two dimensions are very useful in understanding what love is. It is not a romantic momentary sentiment or a story—no. It's concrete, it's in deeds. And it is communicated, that is, it is always in dialogue.

So Chiara, [to return to] your question: "Often we feel disappointed in love. What does the greatness of Jesus' love consist in? How can we experience his love?" And now, I know that you are good and will permit me to speak sincerely. I don't want to be a moralist but I would like to say a word that isn't liked, an unpopular word. Sometimes the pope must also take risks to speak the truth. Love is in works, in communicating, but love is very respectful of people, it does not use people, that is, *love is chaste*. And to you young people in this world, in this hedonistic world, in this world where only pleasure, having a good time, and living the good life get publicity, I say to you: be chaste, be chaste.

All of us in life have gone through moments in which this virtue has been very difficult, but it is in fact the way of genuine love, of a love that is able to give life, that does not seek to use the other for one's own pleasure. It is a love that considers the life of the other person sacred: "I respect you, I don't want to use you." It's not easy. We all know the difficulties in overcoming the "care-free" and hedonistic conception of love. Forgive me if I say something you weren't expecting, but I ask you: strive to experience love chastely.

And from this we draw a conclusion: if love is respectful, if love is in deeds, if love is in communicating, *love makes sacrifices for others*. Look at the love of parents, of so many mothers, of so many fathers who in the morning arrive at work tired because they haven't slept well in order to look after their sick child—this is love! This is respect. This is not having a good time. This is—let's go to another key word—this is *"service." Love is service*. It is serving others. When, after the washing of the feet, Jesus explained the gesture to the apostles, he taught that we are made to serve one another, and if I say that I love but I don't serve the other, don't help the other, don't enable that person to go forward, don't sacrifice myself for him or her, this isn't love. You have carried the Cross [the World Youth Day Cross]:

there is the sign of love. That history of God's love involved
in works and dialogue, with respect, with forgiveness, with
patience during so many centuries of history with his people, ends there—his Son on the cross, the greatest service,
which is giving one's life, sacrificing oneself, helping others. It's not easy to speak of love, it's not easy to experience
love. However, with these things that I have said, Chiara, I
have tried to respond to the question you asked me. I don't
know, but I hope I have been of help to you.

True Friends, True Happiness

Meeting with Young People
Asunción, Paraguay, July 12, 2015

Dear Young People,

I am happy to be with you in this atmosphere of celebration. Happy to listen to your witness and to share your enthusiasm and love for Jesus.

To answer your questions, I would like to speak about some of the things you shared. Manuel, you told us something like this: "Today I really want to serve others, I want to be more generous." You have experienced hard times, and very painful situations, but today you really want to help others, to go out and share your love with others.

Liz, it is not easy to be a mother to your own parents, all the more when you are young, but what great wisdom and maturity your words showed, when you said: "Today I play with her, I change her diapers. These are all things I hand over to God today, but I am barely making up for everything my mother did for me."

You, young Paraguayans, you certainly show great goodness and courage. You also shared how you have tried to move forward. Where you found strength. Both of you said it was in your parish. In your friends from the parish and in the spiritual retreats organized there. These two things are key: friends and spiritual retreats.

Friendship is one of the greatest gifts which a person, a young person, can have and can offer. It really is. How hard it is to live without friends! Think about it: isn't it one of the most beautiful things that Jesus tells us? He says: "I have called you friends, for all that I have heard from my Father I have made known to you" (Jn 15:15). One of the most precious things about our being Christians is that we are friends, friends of Jesus. When you love someone, you spend time with them, you watch out for them and you help them, you tell them what you are thinking, but also you never abandon them. That's how Jesus is with us; he never abandons us. Friends stand by one another, they help one another, they protect one another. The Lord is like that with us. He is patient with us.

Spiritual retreats: Saint Ignatius has a famous meditation on the two standards. He describes the standard of the devil and then the standard of Christ. It would be like the football jerseys of two different teams. And he asks us which team we want to play for.

In this meditation, he has us imagine what it would be like to belong to one or the other team. It is as if he were asking us: "In this life, which team do you want to play for?"

Saint Ignatius says that the devil, in order to recruit players, promises that those who play on his side will receive riches, honor, glory, and power. They will be famous. Everyone will worship them.

Then, Ignatius tells us, there is the way Jesus plays. His game is not something fantastic. Jesus doesn't tell us that we will be stars, celebrities, in this life. Instead, he tells us that playing with him is about humility, love, service to others. Jesus does not lie to us; he takes us seriously.

In the Bible, the devil is called the father of lies. What he promises, or better, what he makes you believe, is that, if you do certain things, you will be happy. And later, when you think about it, you realize that you weren't happy at all. That you were up against something which, far from giving you happiness, made you feel more empty, even sad. Friends, the devil is a con artist. He makes promise after promise, but he never delivers. He'll never really do anything he says. He doesn't make good on his promises. He makes you want things which he can't give...He makes you put your hopes in things that will never make you happy. That's his game, his strategy. He talks a lot, he offers a lot, but he doesn't deliver. He is a con artist because everything he promises us is divisive; it is about comparing ourselves to others, about stepping over them in order to get what we want. He is a con artist because he tells us that we have to abandon our friends, and never to stand by anyone. Everything is based on appearances. He makes us think that our worth depends on how much we possess.

Then we have Jesus, who asks us to play on his team. He doesn't con us, nor does he promise us the world. He doesn't tell us that we will find happiness in wealth, power, and pride. Just the opposite. He shows us a different way. This coach tells his players: "Blessed, happy are the poor in spirit, those who mourn, the meek, those who hunger and thirst for righteousness, the merciful, the pure in heart, the peacemakers, those who are persecuted for righteousness' sake." And he ends up by telling them: "Rejoice on account of all this!"

Why? Because Jesus doesn't lie to us. He shows us a path that is life and truth. He is the great proof of this. His style, his way of living, is friendship, relationship with his Father. And that is what he offers us. He makes us realize that we are sons and daughters. Beloved children.

He does not trick you. He knows that happiness, true happiness, the happiness that can fill our hearts, is not found in designer clothing, or expensive brand-name shoes. He knows that real happiness is found in drawing near to others, learning how to weep with those who weep, being close to those who are feeling low or in trouble, giving them a shoulder to cry on, a hug. If we don't know how to weep, we don't know how to laugh either, we don't know how to live.

Jesus knows that in this world filled with competition, envy, and aggression, true happiness comes from learning to be patient, from respecting others, from refusing to condemn or judge others. As the saying goes: "When you get angry, you lose." Don't let your heart give in to anger and resentment. Happy are the merciful. Happy are those who know how to put themselves in someone else's shoes, those who are able to embrace, to forgive. We have all experienced this at one time or another. And how beautiful it is! It is like getting our lives back, getting a new chance. Nothing is more beautiful than to have a new chance. It is as if life can start all over again.

Happy too are those who bring new life and new opportunities. Happy those who work and sacrifice to do this. All of us have made mistakes and been caught up in misunderstandings, a thousand of them. Happy, then, are those who can help others when they make mistakes, when they experience misunderstandings. They are true friends, they do not give up on anyone. They are the pure of heart, the ones who can look beyond the little things and overcome difficulties. Happy above all are the ones who can see the good in other people.

The saints are our friends and models. They no longer play on our field, but we continue to look to them in our efforts to play our best game. They show us that Jesus is no con artist; he offers us genuine fulfillment. But above all, he offers us friendship, true friendship, the friendship we all need.

So we need to be friends the way Jesus is a friend. Not to be closed in on ourselves, but to join his team and play his game, to go out and make more and more friends. To bring the excitement of Jesus' friendship to the world. And you can do this wherever you find yourselves: at work, at school, on WhatsApp, Facebook, or Twitter. When you go out dancing, or for a drink of *tereré*, when you meet in the town square or play a little match on the neighborhood field. That is where Jesus' friends can be found. And being friends is not a matter of conning others, but of standing beside them and being patient with them—with the patience that comes from knowing that we are happy, because we have a Father who is in heaven.

The Path of Hope

Address to Students
Fr. Félix Varela Cultural Center, Havana, Cuba
September 20, 2015

Dear Friends,

I am very happy to be with you here in this cultural center which is so important in Cuban history. I thank God for this opportunity to meet so many young people who, by their work, studies, and training, are dreaming of—and already making real—the future of Cuba.

What kind of hope does a young Cuban have at this moment in history? Nothing more or less than that of any other young person in any other part of the world. Because hope speaks to us of something deeply rooted in every human heart, independent of our concrete circumstances and historical conditioning. Hope speaks to us of a thirst, an aspiration, a longing for a life of fulfillment, a desire to achieve great things, things that fill our heart and lift our spirit to lofty realities like truth, goodness and beauty, justice and love. But it also involves taking risks. It means being ready to not be seduced by what is fleeting, by false promises of happiness, by immediate and selfish pleasures,

62

by a life of mediocrity and self-centeredness, which only fills the heart with sadness and bitterness. No, hope is bold; it can look beyond personal convenience, the petty securities and compensations that limit our horizon; it can open us up to grand ideals that make life more beautiful and worthwhile. I would ask each one of you: What is it that shapes your life? What lies deep in your heart? Where do your hopes and aspirations lie? Are you ready to put yourself on the line for the sake of something even greater?

But what are we to do? How do we find paths of hope in the situations in which we live? How do we make those hopes for fulfillment, authenticity, justice, and truth become a reality in our personal lives, in our country, and in our world? I think that there are three ideas that can help to keep our hope alive:

Hope is a path made of memory and discernment. Hope is the virtue that goes places. It isn't simply a road we take for the pleasure of it, but it has an end, a goal that is practical and lights our way. Hope is also nourished by memory; it looks not only to the future but also to the past and present. To keep moving forward in life, in addition to knowing where we want to go, we also need to know who we are and where we come from. Individuals or peoples who have no memory and erase their past risk losing their identity and destroying their future. So we need to remember who we are, and in what our spiritual and moral heritage consists. Discernment is also needed, because it is essential to be open to reality and to be able to interpret it without fear or prejudice. Partial and ideological interpretations are useless; they only deform reality by trying to fit it into our preconceived notions, and they always cause disappointment and despair. We need discernment and memory, because discernment is not blind; it is built on solid ethical and moral criteria that help us to see what is good and just.

Hope is a path taken with others. An African proverb says: "If you want to go fast, go alone; if you want to go far, go with others." Isolation and aloofness never generate hope; but closeness to others and encounter do. Left to ourselves, we will go nowhere. Nor by exclusion will we be able to build a future for anyone, even ourselves. A path of hope calls for a culture of encounter and dialogue that can overcome conflict and sterile confrontation. To create that culture, it is vital to see different ways of thinking in terms not of risk but of richness and growth. The world needs this culture of encounter. It needs young people who seek to know and love one another, who seek to journey together in building a country like that which José Martí dreamed of: "With all, and for the good of all."

Hope is a path of solidarity. The culture of encounter should naturally lead to a culture of solidarity. Without solidarity, no country has a future. Beyond all other considerations or interests, there has to be concern for that person who may be my friend, my companion, but also for someone who may think differently from the way I do, someone with his own ideas yet just as human and just as Cuban as I am. Simple tolerance is not enough; we have to go well beyond that, passing from a suspicious and defensive attitude to one of acceptance, cooperation, concrete service, and effective assistance. Do not be afraid of solidarity, service, and offering a helping hand, so that no one is excluded from the path.

This path of life is lit up by a higher hope, the hope born of our faith in Christ. He made himself our companion along the way. Not only does he encourage us, he also accompanies us; he is at our side and he extends a friendly hand to us. The Son of God, he wanted to become someone like us, to accompany us on our way. Faith in his presence, in his friendship and love, lights up all our hopes and dreams. With him at our side, we learn to discern what is real, to encounter and serve others, and to walk the path of solidarity.

Dear young people of Cuba, if God himself entered our history and became flesh in Jesus, if he shouldered our weakness and sin, then you need not be afraid of hope, or of the future, because God is on your side. He believes in you, and he hopes in you.

Overcoming Fears

Meeting with Young People
Kololo Air Strip, Kampala, Uganda, November 28, 2015

Dear Young Friends,

I am happy to be here and to share these moments with you. Today, if you will allow me, I want to confirm you in your faith, encourage you in your love, and in a special way, strengthen you in your hope.

Christian hope is not simply optimism; it is much more. It is rooted in the new life we have received in Jesus Christ. Saint Paul tells us that hope will not disappoint us, because God's love was poured into our hearts by the Holy Spirit at our baptism (cf. Rom 5:5). This hope enables us to trust in Christ's promises, to trust in the power of his love, his forgiveness, his friendship. That love opens the door to new life. Whenever you experience a problem, a setback, a failure, you must anchor your heart in that love, for it has the power to turn death into life and to banish every evil.

So this afternoon I would invite you, first of all, to pray for this gift to grow within you, and for the grace to become messengers of hope. There are so many people around us who experience deep anxiety and even despair. Jesus lifts these clouds, if we allow him to.

I would also like to share with you a few thoughts about some of the obstacles you may encounter on our journey of hope. All of you want a better future, employment, health, and prosperity. This is good. You want to share your gifts, your aspirations, and your enthusiasm with others, for the good of the nation and of the Church. This too is very good. But when you see poverty, when you experience lack of opportunity, when you experience failure in your lives, sometimes a feeling of despair can grow. You can be tempted to lose hope.

Have you ever seen a little child who stops in front of a dirty puddle on the path ahead of him? A puddle he cannot leap over or go around? He may try but then he stumbles and gets soaked. Then, after many attempts, he calls out to his father, who takes his hand and swings him over to the other side. We are like that child. Life presents us with many dirty puddles. But we don't have to overcome all those problems and hurdles on our own. God is there to take our hand, if only we call on him.

What I am saying is that all of us have to be like that little child—even the pope! For it is only when we are small and humble that we are not afraid to call out to our Father. If you have experienced his help, you know what I am speaking about. We need to learn to put our hope in him, knowing that he is always there for us. He gives us confidence and courage. But—and this is important—it would be wrong not to share this beautiful experience with others. It would be wrong for us not to become messengers of hope for others.

There is one particular puddle that can be frightening to young people who want to grow in their friendship with Christ. It is the fear of failing in our commitment to love, and above all, failing in that great and lofty ideal that is Christian marriage. You may be afraid of failing to be a good wife and mother, failing to be a good husband and father. If you are looking at that puddle, you may even see your weaknesses and fears reflected back to you. Please, don't give in to them! Sometimes these fears come from the devil who does not want you to be happy. No! Call out to God, extend your hearts to him and he will lift you in his arms and show you how to love. I ask young couples in particular to trust that God wants to bless their love and their lives with his grace in the sacrament of marriage. At the heart of Christian marriage is God's gift of love, not the costly parties that often obscure the deep spiritual meaning of this day of joyful celebration with family and friends.

Finally, one puddle that we all have to face is the fear of being different, of going against the grain in a society that puts increasing pressure on us to embrace models of gratification and consumption alien to the deepest values of African culture. Think about it! What would the Uganda martyrs say about the misuse of our modern means of communication, where young people are exposed to images and distorted views of sexuality that degrade human dignity, leading to sadness and emptiness? What would be the Uganda martyrs' reaction to the growth of greed and corruption in our midst? Surely they would appeal to you to be model Christians, confident that your love of Christ, your fidelity to the Gospel, and your wise use of your God-given gifts can only enrich, purify, and elevate the life of this country. The Uganda martyrs continue to show you the way. Do not be afraid to let the light of your faith shine in your families, your schools, and your places of work. Do not be afraid to enter into dialogue humbly with others who may see things differently.

Courage and Resilience

Prayer Vigil with Young People
Cathedral Square, Bangui, Central African Republic
November 29, 2015

Dear Young Friends,

I greet all of you with affection. Your friend who spoke in your name said that your symbol is the banana tree, because it is a symbol of life: banana trees keep growing, they spread, they bear fruit that always gives nourishment and strength. Banana trees are also resilient. I think that this is clearly the path set out before you in this difficult time of war, hatred, and division: it is the road of resilience.

Your friend said that some of you want to leave home. Fleeing from life's challenges is never a solution! It is necessary to be resilient, to have the courage to resist, to fight for what is right! Those who flee do not have the courage to give life. Banana trees give life, they spread and keep giving new life because they are resilient, they remain, they stay put. Some of you will say: "But Father, what can we do? How can we be resilient?" Let me share with you two or three thoughts that may be helpful to you in being resilient.

First of all, *prayer*. Prayer is powerful! Prayer conquers evil! Prayer makes you draw near to God who is all-powerful. Let me ask you a question: Do you pray? I can't hear you!

[*Yes!*]

Don't forget this!

Second, *work for peace*. Peace is not a document that gets signed and then filed away. Peace is built day by day! And peace is crafted; it is the work of our hands; it is built up by the way we live our lives. But someone may say: "Tell me, Father, how can I build peace? How can I be a peacemaker?" First: never hate anyone. If someone wrongs you, seek to forgive. No hatred! Much forgiveness! Let us all say this together: "No hatred! Much forgiveness!"

[*All repeat*]

And if hatred does not dwell in your heart, if you forgive, then you will be a winner. Because you will win the hardest battle in life; you will win in love. And from love comes peace.

Do you want to be winners or losers in life? What do you want?

[*We want to be winners!*]

But we win only if we take the road of love. The road of love. Can we love our enemies?

[*Yes!*]

Can we forgive those who do us wrong?

[*Yes!*]

So, through love and forgiveness, you will be winners. With love you will win in life and you will always give life. Love will never make you losers.

Now I wish you all the best. Think of the banana tree. Think of resilience in the face of problems. Fleeing, going away is not a solution. You must be courageous. Have you understood what it means to be courageous? Courageous in forgiving, courageous in loving, courageous in building peace. Is that right?

[*Yes!*]

Let's say it together! "Courageous in love, in forgiveness, in building peace."

You Are the Wealth of the Church

Meeting with Young People
"José María Morelos y Pavón" Stadium, Morelia, Mexico
February 16, 2016

I have to tell you that when I arrived in this country I received a warm welcome and I saw something that I have known for a long time: the vitality, the joy, and the festive spirit of the Mexican people. *Ahorita* [and now]...after listening to you, but particularly after seeing you, I am also certain about something else. One of Mexico's greatest treasures is that it has a youthful face: its young people. Yes, you are the wealth of this land. Notice that I didn't say the hope of this land, but its wealth.

The mountain may have rich minerals to serve humanity's advancement, in terms of its wealth, but that richness has to be converted into hope by hard work, just as miners do when they extract those minerals. You are this wealth, and it has to be converted into hope. Hope is born when you are able to feel that all is not lost; and for this to happen it is necessary to start "at home," to begin with yourself. Not everything is lost. I am not lost; I am worth something, I am worth a lot.

The biggest threat to hope is when you feel that you do not matter to anybody or that you have been left aside. This is the great obstacle to hope: when, in a family, society, school, or group of friends, you are made to feel unimportant. This is hard and painful, but it does happen, am I right? Yes or no?

["*Yes!*"]

Yes, it happens. This kills, this crushes us and opens the door to much suffering. But there is also another big threat to the hope that your richness will grow and bear fruit, and it is this: to allow yourself to believe that you begin to be valuable when you start wearing the right clothes, the latest brands and fashions, or when you start enjoying prestige and importance because you have money—but in the depths of your heart you do not believe that you are worthy of kindness or love and this is something that your heart intuits. Hope is silenced by what they make you believe, and they don't let you flourish. The biggest threat is when a person feels that he or she must have money to buy everything, including the love of others. The biggest threat is to believe that by having a big car you will be happy. Is this true, that by having a big car you will be happy?

["*No!*"]

You are the wealth of Mexico, you are the wealth of the Church.

You have asked me for a word of hope, and the one word I have to give you, which is the foundation of everything, is Jesus Christ. When everything seems too much, when it seems that the world is crashing down on you, embrace his cross, draw close to him and please, never let go of his hand, even if they are dragging you; and, if you should fall, allow him to lift you up. Mountain climbers have a lovely song that I like to repeat to young people. As they go up the mountain they sing: "In the art of climbing upwards, the triumph is not in not falling but rather in not staying down on the ground."

This is the art, and, who is the only one who can take you by the hand so that you are not left lying on the ground? Jesus Christ is the only one. Jesus Christ, who sometimes sends a brother or sister to speak to you or to help you. Don't hide your hand when you have fallen, do not say to him: "Don't look at me, I am covered in mud. Don't look at me, I am without hope." You have only to let him take hold of your hand and you of his, and then that richness which is inside you, which is covered in mud, and which you have given up on, will begin, through hope, to bear fruit. But always holding onto Jesus' hand. This is the way, do not forget: "In the art of climbing upwards, the triumph is not in not falling but rather in not staying down on the ground."

Never allow yourselves to stay down, fallen on the ground! Never! Agreed? And if you see a friend who has slipped up in life and fallen, go and offer him or her your hand, but do so with respect for their dignity. Put yourself on their level, listen to them and don't say: "I have the solution for you." No, as a friend, slowly give them strength by your words, give them strength by your listening, that medicine which sadly is being forgotten: "listening ther-apy." Let them speak, let them share their experience, and then, little by little, they will offer you their hand, and, in the name of Jesus Christ, you can help them. But if you go in suddenly and begin to give them a sermon, going on about the same thing, well then, they will be worse off than before. Am I clear?

["*Yes!*"]

Never let go of Jesus' hand, never leave him. And if you do move away from him, get up and keep moving forward; he understands what you are going through. Hand in hand with Jesus it is possible to live fully, by holding his hand it is possible to believe that life is worth the effort, it is worth giving of your best, to be leaven, salt, and light among friends, in neighborhoods, communities, and families.

Of course, on this journey you may perhaps not be able to have the model car, you will not have pockets filled with money, but you will have something that no one can take away from you, which is the experience of being loved, em-braced, and accompanied. It is the delight of enjoying an encounter, the delight of dreaming and desiring encounter among everyone. It is the experience of being family, of feel-ing oneself as part of a community. It is the experience of being able to look the world in the face, with your head held up high, without the car, without the money, but with your head held high: this is dignity. Three words we want to repeat: value, because you have been made valuable; hope, because we want to be open to hope; and dignity. Let us repeat these three words: value, hope, and dignity. It is the value, the worth that God has given you. You are the wealth of Mexico. The hope and dignity that Jesus Christ gives you means not allowing yourselves to be manipulated and not allowing yourselves to be used as commodities to fill the pockets of other people.

Dear brothers and sisters, you are the wealth of this country, and when you doubt this, look to Jesus Christ, who is the hope, the one who destroys all efforts to make you worthless or mere instruments of other people's ambitions.

Do Not Raise Walls of Division

Video Message to the Youth of Canada
October 22, 2017

Dear young Canadian friends!

I'm happy to be able to spend a little time with you, participating in your dialogue, in which you are participating from the Atlantic to the Pacific. There are these marvels of technology that, if used positively, provide an opportunity for encounter and exchange unthinkable until recently.

This confirms that, when people work together looking for each other's good, the world reveals itself in all its beauty. I ask you, therefore, not to let the world be ruined by those without scruples, who think only about exploiting it and destroying it. I invite you to flood the places where you live with the joy and enthusiasm typical of your youthful age, to irrigate the world and history with the joy that comes from the Gospel, from having met a Person: Jesus, who has enthralled you and has drawn you to be with him.

Do not let your youth be stolen from you. Do not allow anyone to slow and obscure the light that Christ puts in your face and in your heart. Be weavers of relationships signed by trust, by sharing, by openness even to ends of the world. Do not raise walls of division. Do not raise walls of division! Build bridges, like this extraordinary one that you are crossing in spirit, and that links the shores of two oceans. You are experiencing a moment of intense preparation for the next synod—the Synod of Bishops—one that concerns you in a particular way, just as it involves the whole Christian community. In fact, its theme is "Young People, Faith and Vocational Discernment."

I also want to remind you of Jesus' words, those he said one day to the disciples who asked him, "Rabbi, where do you live?" And Jesus answered, "Come and see." Jesus also turns his gaze on you and invites you to go to him. Dear young people, have you encountered this gaze? Have you heard this voice? Have you felt that impulse to get up and be on the way? I am sure that, although din and dizziness seem to reign in the world, this call continues to resonate in your soul, to open it to full joy. This will be possible to the extent that you, with the accompaniment of expert guides, undertake an itinerary of discernment in order to discover God's plan for your life: yours, yours, yours, and yours—the plan he has for the life of each one of you—even when your journey is marked by danger and missteps, God, rich in mercy, reaches out his hand to pick you up again...

The world and the Church are in need of courageous young people who are not cowed in the face of difficulties, who face their trials and keep their eyes and hearts open to reality, so that no one should be rejected, or subjected to injustice or to violence, or deprived of human dignity.

I'm sure your heart—a young heart—will not be closed to the cry for help of so many of your peers who seek freedom, work, study, a chance to make sense of their lives. I count on your willingness, your commitment, your ability to face important challenges and dare to make the future, to take decisive steps along the path of change.

Young people, let Christ reach you. Let him speak to you, embrace you, console you, heal your wounds, dissolve your doubts and fears—and you shall be ready for the fascinating adventure of life, that precious and inestimable gift that God places every day in your hands. Go to meet Jesus, be with him in prayer, entrust yourselves to him, give your whole life over to his merciful love; then your faith, and your faith will be the luminous witness of generosity and of the joy there is in following him, wherever he may lead you.

Dear young people of Canada, my hope for you is that your meeting should be like that of the first disciples, that the beauty of a life realized in following the Lord might open wide before you. For this reason I entrust you to Mary of Nazareth, a young person like you, to whom God turned his loving gaze, that he might take you by the hand. Let yourselves be taken by Mary, and let her guide you to the joy of saying a full and generous, "Here I am!"

Jesus watches you and awaits a "Here I am!" from each of you.

I bless you, I embrace you, and I greet you with affection while I ask you, please, to pray for me, so that I may be a faithful cooperator with your joy. Thank you.

WORLD YOUTH DAYS

A Window on the Future

Welcome Ceremony
Garden of Guanabara Palace, Rio de Janeiro, July 22, 2013

As you know, the principal reason for my visit to Brazil goes beyond its borders. I have actually come for World Youth Day. I am here to meet young people coming from all over the world, drawn to the open arms of Christ the Redeemer. They want to find a refuge in his embrace, close to his heart, to listen again to his clear and powerful appeal: "Go and make disciples of all nations."

These young people are from every continent, they speak many languages, they bring with them different cultures, and yet they also find in Christ the answer to their highest aspirations, held in common, and they can satisfy the hunger for a pure truth and an authentic love that binds them together in spite of differences.

Christ offers them space, knowing that there is no force more powerful than the one released from the hearts of young people when they have been conquered by the experience of friendship with him. Christ has confidence in young people and entrusts them with the very future of his mission, "Go and make disciples." Go beyond the confines of what is humanly possible and create a world of brothers and sisters! And young people have confidence in Christ: they are not afraid to risk for him the only life they have, because they know they will not be disappointed.

As I begin my visit to Brazil, I am well aware that, in addressing young people, I am also speaking to their families, their local and national church communities, the societies they come from, and the men and women upon whom this new generation largely depends.

Here it is common for parents to say, "Our children are the apple of our eye." What a beautiful expression of Brazilian wisdom this is, applying to young people an image referring to the eye, which is the window through which light enters into us, granting us the miracle of sight! What would become of us if we didn't look after our eyes? How could we move forward? I hope that, during this week, each one of us will ask ourselves this thought-provoking question.

Listen! Young people are the window through which the future enters the world. They are the window, and so they present us with great challenges. Our generation will show that it can rise to the promise found in each young person when we know how to give our children space. This means that we have to create the material and spiritual conditions for their full development; to give them a solid basis on which to build their lives; to guarantee their safety and their education to be everything they can be; to pass on to them lasting values that make life worth living; to provide for them a transcendent horizon in their thirst for authentic happiness and their creativity for the good; to endow them with the legacy of a world worthy of human life; and to awaken in them their greatest potential as builders of their own destiny, sharing responsibility for the future of everyone. If we can do all this, we anticipate today the future that enters the world through the window of the young.

Make Yourself Heard

Meeting with Young People from Argentina
Cathedral of Saint Sebastian, Rio de Janeiro, July 25, 2013

Let me tell you what I hope will be the outcome of World Youth Day: I hope there will be noise. Here there will be noise, I'm quite sure. Here in Rio there will be plenty of noise, no doubt about that. But I want you to make yourselves heard in your dioceses, I want your voices to go out, I want the Church to go out into the streets, I want us to resist everything worldly, everything static, everything comfortable, everything to do with clericalism, everything that might make us closed in on ourselves. The parishes, the schools, the institutions are made for going out...if they don't, they become NGOs [non-governmental organizations], and the Church cannot be an NGO. May the bishops and priests forgive me if some of you create a bit of confusion afterwards. That's my advice. Thanks for whatever you can do.

Look, at this moment, I think our world civilization has gone beyond its limits. It has gone beyond its limits because it has made money into such a god that we are now faced with a philosophy, a practice, that excludes the two ends of life that are most full of promise for people. It excludes the elderly, obviously. You could easily think there is a kind of hidden euthanasia, that is, we don't take care of the elderly; but there is also a cultural euthanasia, because we don't allow them to speak, we don't allow them to act. And there is the exclusion of the young. The percentage of our young people without work, without employment, is very high, and we have a generation with no experience of the dignity gained through work. This civilization, in other words, has led us to exclude the two peaks that make up our future. As for the young, they must emerge, they must assert themselves. The young must go out to fight for values, to fight for these values. And the elderly must open their mouths, the elderly must open their mouths and teach us! Pass on to us the wisdom of the peoples!

Among the Argentine people, I ask the elderly, from my heart: do not cease to be the cultural storehouse of our people, a storehouse that hands on justice, hands on history, hands on values, hands on the memory of the people. And the rest of you, please, do not oppose the elderly: let them speak, listen to them and go forward. But know this, know that at this moment, you young people and you elderly people are condemned to the same destiny: exclusion. Don't allow yourselves to be excluded. It's obvious! You must work to resist exclusion.

Faith in Jesus Christ is not a joke, it is something very serious. It is a scandal that God came to be one of us. It is a scandal that he died on a cross. It is a scandal: the scandal of the cross. The cross continues to provoke scandal. But it is the one sure path, the path of the cross, the path of Jesus, the path of the incarnation of Jesus. Please do not water down your faith in Jesus Christ. We dilute fruit drinks—orange, apple, or banana juice—but please do not drink a diluted form of faith. Faith is whole and entire, not something that you water down. It is faith in Jesus. It is faith in the Son of God made man, who loved me and who died for me. So then: make yourselves heard; take care of the two ends of the population, the elderly and the young; do not allow yourselves to be excluded and do not allow the elderly to be excluded.

Second: do not "water down" your faith in Jesus Christ. Consider the Beatitudes. What must we do, Father? Look, read the Beatitudes: that will do you good. If you want to know what you actually have to do, read Matthew, chapter 25, which is the standard by which we will be judged. With these two things you have the action plan: the Beatitudes and Matthew 25. You do not need to read anything else. I ask you this with all my heart. But do not forget: make yourselves heard. Take care of the two ends of life, the two ends of the history of peoples: the elderly and the young; and do not water down the faith. And now let us pray, so as to bless the image of the Virgin, and then I will bless you.

Put on Faith!

Welcoming Ceremony for Young People
Waterfront of Copacabana, Rio de Janeiro, July 25, 2013

Dear Young Friends,

Good evening! First of all, I want to thank you for the testimony you are giving to the world. I always heard it said that the people of Rio didn't like the cold and rain, but you are showing that your faith is stronger than the cold and rain. Congratulations! You are true heroes!

In you I see the beauty of Christ's young face and I am filled with joy. I recall the first international World Youth. It was celebrated in 1987 in Argentina, in my home city of Buenos Aires. I still cherish the words of Blessed John Paul II to the young people on that occasion: "I have great hope in you! I hope above all that you will renew your fidelity to Jesus Christ and to his redeeming cross" (Address to Young People, Buenos Aires, April 11, 1987).

This year, World Youth Day comes to Latin America for the second time. I am looking at the large crowd before me—there are so many of you! And you have come from every continent! In many cases you have come from afar, not only geographically, but also existentially, culturally, socially, and humanly. But today you are all here, or—better yet—we are all here together as one, in order to share the faith and the joy of an encounter with Christ, of being his disciples. This week Rio has become the center of the Church, its heart both youthful and vibrant, because you have responded generously and courageously to the invitation that Christ has made to you to be with him and to become his friends.

The train of this World Youth Day has come from afar and has traveled across all of Brazil following the stages of the project entitled *"Bota fé*—put on faith!" Today the train has arrived at Rio de Janeiro. From Corcovado, Christ the Redeemer embraces us and blesses us. Looking out to this sea, the beach and all of you gathered here, I am reminded of the moment when Jesus called the first disciples to follow him by the shores of Lake Tiberias. Today Christ asks each of us again: Do you want to be my disciple? Do you want to be my friend? Do you want to be a witness to my Gospel? In the spirit of the Year of Faith, these questions invite us to renew our commitment as Christians.

Your families and local communities have passed on to you the great gift of faith. Christ has grown in you. Today he desires to come here to confirm you in this faith, faith in the living Christ who dwells within you. But I have come as well to be confirmed by the enthusiasm of your faith! You know that in the life of a bishop there are many problems that need to be resolved. And with these problems and difficulties, a bishop's faith can grow sad. How horrible is a sad bishop! How bad is that! So that my faith might not be sad, I came here to be filled with your contagious enthusiasm!

I greet you with affection. All of you assembled here from the five continents and, through you, all young people of the world, in particular those who wanted to come to Rio de Janeiro but weren't able to come. To those who are following us by means of radio, television and the internet, to everyone I say: Welcome to this feast of faith! In several parts of the world, at this very moment, many young people have come together to share this event with us. Let us all experience the joy of being united with each other in friendship and faith. And be sure of this: my heart embraces all of you with universal affection. Because what is most important today is your gathering here and the gathering together of all the young people who are following us through various forms of media. From the summit of the mountain of Corcovado, Christ the Redeemer welcomes you and embraces you in this beautiful city of Rio!

HOMILY OF THE HOLY FATHER

Dear Friends,

"It is good for us to be here!" Peter cries out after seeing the Lord Jesus transfigured in glory. Are we able to repeat these words with him? I think the answer is yes, because here today, it is good for all of us to be together around Jesus! It is he who welcomes us and who is present in our midst here in Rio. In the Gospel we have heard God the Father say: "This is my Son, my chosen one; listen to him!" (Lk 9:35). If it is Jesus who welcomes us, we too want to welcome him and listen to his words. It is precisely through the welcome we give to Jesus Christ, the Word made flesh, that the Holy Spirit transforms us, lights up our way to the future, and enables us joyfully to advance along that way with wings of hope (cf. *Lumen Fidei*, 7).

But what can we do? "*Bota fé*—put on faith." The World Youth Day Cross has proclaimed these words in its pilgrimage throughout Brazil. "Put on faith": what does this mean? When we prepare a plate of food and we see that it needs salt, well, we "put on" salt; when it needs oil, then we "put on" oil. "To put on," that is, to place on top of, to pour over. And so it is in our life, dear young friends. If we want it to have real meaning and fulfillment, as you want and as you deserve, I say to each one of you, "Put on faith," and life will take on a new flavor, life will have a compass to show you the way; "put on hope" and every one of your days will be enlightened and your horizon will no longer be dark, but luminous; "put on love," and your life will be like a house built on rock, your journey will be joyful, because you will find many friends to journey with you. Put on faith, put on hope, put on love! All together: "put on faith," "put on hope," "put on love."

But who can give us all this? In the Gospel we hear the answer: Christ. "This is my Son, my chosen one. Listen to him!" Jesus brings God to us and us to God. With him, our life is transformed and renewed, and we can see reality with new eyes, from Jesus' standpoint, with his own eyes (cf. *Lumen Fidei*, 18). For this reason, I say to every one of you today: "Put on Christ" in your life, and you will find a friend in whom you can always trust. "Put on Christ" and you will see the wings of hope spreading and letting you journey with joy toward the future. "Put on Christ" and your life will be full of his love; it will be a fruitful life. And we all want to have a fruitful life, one that is life-giving for others.

Today, it would be good for all of us to ask ourselves honestly: In whom do we place our trust? In ourselves, in material things, or in Jesus? We all often have the temptation to put ourselves at the center, to believe that we are the axis of the universe, to believe that we alone build our lives or to think that our lives can only be happy if they are built on possessions, money, or power. But we all know that this is not so. Certainly, possessions, money, and power can provide a momentary thrill, the illusion of being happy, but they end up possessing us and making us always want to have more, so that we are never satisfied. We end up "full" but not nourished, and it is very sad to see young people "full" but weak. Young people must be strong, nourished by the faith and not filled with other things! "Put on Christ" in your life, place your trust in him and you will never be disappointed!

You see how faith accomplishes a revolution in us, one that we can call Copernican; it removes us from the center and puts God at the center. Faith immerses us in his love and gives us security, strength, and hope. Seemingly, nothing has changed. Yet, in the depths of our being, everything is different. With God, peace, consolation, gentleness, courage, serenity, and joy, which are all fruits of the Holy Spirit (cf. Gal 5:22), find a home in our heart. Then our very being is transformed; our way of thinking and acting is made new, it becomes Jesus' own way of thinking and acting. Dear friends, faith is revolutionary, and today I ask you: Are you open to entering into this revolutionary wave of faith? Only by entering into this wave will your young lives make sense and so be fruitful!

Dear young people: "Put on Christ" in your lives. In these days, Christ awaits you in his word; listen carefully to him and his presence will arouse your heart. "Put on Christ": he awaits you in the sacrament of penance, with his mercy he will cure all the wounds caused by sin. Do not be afraid to ask God's forgiveness, because he never tires of forgiving us, like a father who loves us. God is pure mercy! "Put on Christ": he is waiting for you also in the Eucharist, the sacrament of his presence and his sacrifice of love, and he is waiting for you also in the humanity of the many young people who will enrich you with their friendship, encourage you by their witness to the faith, and teach you the language of love, goodness, and service.

You too, dear young people, can be joyful witnesses of his love, courageous witnesses of his Gospel, carrying to this world a ray of his light. Let yourselves be loved by Christ, he is a friend who will not disappoint.

"It is good for us to be here," putting on Christ in our lives, putting on the faith, hope, and love that he gives us. Dear friends, in this celebration we have welcomed the image of Our Lady of Aparecida. In our prayer to Mary, we ask her to teach us to follow Jesus, that she may teach us to be disciples and missionaries. Like her, may we say "Yes" to God. Let us ask that her maternal heart intercede for us, so that our hearts may be open to loving Jesus and bring others to love him. Dear young people, Jesus is waiting for us. Jesus is counting on us. Amen.

Questions of the Cross

Way of the Cross with Young People
Waterfront of Copacabana, Rio de Janeiro
July 26, 2013

Dear Young Friends,

We have come here today to accompany Jesus on his journey of sorrow and love, the Way of the Cross, which is one of the most intense moments of World Youth Day. At the end of the Holy Year of Redemption, Blessed John Paul II chose to entrust the Cross to you, young people, asking you "to carry it throughout the world as a symbol of Christ's love for humanity, and announce to everyone that only in the death and resurrection of Christ can we find salvation and redemption" (Address to Young People, April 22, 1984). Since then, the World Youth Day Cross has traveled to every continent and through a variety of human situations. It is, as it were, almost "steeped" in the life experiences of the countless young people who have seen it and carried it. Dear brothers and sisters, no one can approach and touch the cross of Jesus without leaving something of himself or herself there, and without bringing something of the cross of Jesus into his or her own life.

I have three questions that I hope will echo in your hearts this evening as you walk beside Jesus: What have you left on the cross, dear young people of Brazil, during these two years that it has been crisscrossing your great country? What has the cross of Jesus left for you, in each one of you? Finally, what does this cross teach us?

1. According to an ancient Roman tradition, while fleeing the city during the persecutions of Nero, Saint Peter saw Jesus who was traveling in the opposite direction, that is, toward the city, and asked him in amazement: "Lord, where are you going?" Jesus' response was: "I am going to Rome to be crucified again." At that moment, Peter understood that he had to follow the Lord with courage, to the very end. But he also realized that he would never be alone on the journey; Jesus, who had loved him even unto death, would always be with him. Jesus, with his cross, walks with us and takes upon himself our fears, our problems, and our sufferings, even those that are deepest and most painful. With the cross, Jesus unites himself to the silence of the victims of violence, those who can no longer cry out, especially the innocent and the defenseless; with the cross, he is united to families in trouble and those who mourn the tragic loss of their children, as in the case of the 242 young victims of the fire in the City of Santa Maria at the beginning of this year. We pray for them.

On the cross, Jesus is united with every person who suffers from hunger in a world which, on the other hand, permits itself the luxury of throwing away tons of food every day. On the cross, Jesus is united to the many mothers and fathers who suffer as they see their children become victims of drug-induced euphoria. On the cross, Jesus is united with those who are persecuted for their religion, for their beliefs, or simply for the color of their skin. On the cross, Jesus is united with so many young people who have lost faith in political institutions, because they see in them only selfishness and corruption; he unites himself with those young people who have lost faith in the Church, or even in God, because of the counter-witness of Christians and ministers of the Gospel. How our inconsistencies make Jesus suffer! The cross of Christ bears the suffering and the sin of mankind, including our own. Jesus accepts all this with open arms, bearing on his shoulders our crosses and saying to us: "Have courage! You do not carry your cross alone! I carry it with you. I have overcome death and I have come to give you hope, to give you life" (cf. Jn 3:16).

2. Now we can answer the second question: What has the cross given to those who have gazed upon it and to those who have touched it? What has the cross left in each one of us? You see, it gives us a treasure that no one else can give: the certainty of the faithful love that God has for us—a love so great that it enters into our sin and forgives it, enters into our suffering and gives us the strength to bear it. It is a love that enters into death to conquer it and to save us. The cross of Christ contains all the love of God; there we find his immeasurable mercy. This is a love in which we can place all our trust, in which we can believe. Dear young people, let us entrust ourselves to Jesus, let us give ourselves over to him (cf. *Lumen Fidei*, 16), because he never disappoints anyone! Only in Christ crucified and risen can we find salvation and redemption. With him, evil, suffering, and death

do not have the last word, because he gives us hope and life: he has transformed the cross from being an instrument of hate, defeat, and death to being a sign of love, victory, triumph, and life.

The first name given to Brazil was "The Land of the Holy Cross." The cross of Christ was planted five centuries ago not only on the shores of this country, but also in the history, the hearts, and the lives of the people of Brazil and elsewhere. The suffering Christ is keenly felt here, as one of us who shares our journey even to the end. There is no cross, big or small, in our life, that the Lord does not share with us.

3. But the cross of Christ invites us also to allow ourselves to be smitten by his love, teaching us always to look upon others with mercy and tenderness, especially those who suffer, who are in need of help, who need a word or a concrete action; the cross invites us to step outside ourselves to meet them and to extend a hand to them. How many times have we seen them in the Way of the Cross, how many times have they accompanied Jesus on the way to Calvary: Pilate, Simon of Cyrene, Mary, the women... Today I ask you: Which of them do you want to be? Do you want to be like Pilate, who did not have the courage to go against the tide to save Jesus' life, and instead washed his hands? Tell me: Are you one of those who wash their hands, who feign ignorance and look the other way? Or are you like Simon of Cyrene, who helped Jesus to carry that heavy wood, or like Mary and the other women, who were not afraid to accompany Jesus all the way to the end, with love and tenderness? And you, who do you want to be? Like Pilate? Like

Simon? Like Mary? Jesus is looking at you now and is asking you: Do you want to help me carry the cross? Brothers and sisters, with all the strength of your youth, how will you respond to him?

Dear friends, let us bring to Christ's cross our joys, our sufferings, and our failures. There we will find a Heart that is open to us and understands us, forgives us, loves us, and calls us to bear this love in our lives, to love each person, each brother and sister, with the same love.

The Field of Faith

Prayer Vigil with Young People
Waterfront of Copacabana, Rio de Janeiro
July 27, 2013

Dear Young Friends,

Seeing you all present here today, I think of the story of Saint Francis of Assisi. In front of the crucifix he heard the voice of Jesus saying to him: "Francis, go, rebuild my house." The young Francis responded readily and generously to the Lord's call to rebuild his house. But which house? Slowly but surely, Francis came to realize that it was not a question of repairing a stone building, but about doing his part for the life of the Church. It was a matter of being at the service of the Church, loving her and working to make the countenance of Christ shine ever more brightly in her.

Today too, as always, the Lord needs you, young people, for his Church. My friends, the Lord needs you! Today too, he is calling each of you to follow him in his Church and to be missionaries. The Lord is calling you today! Not the masses, but you, and you, and you—each one of you. Listen to what he is saying to you in your heart. I think that we can learn something from what has taken place in these days, from how we had to cancel, due to bad weather, this vigil in the *Campus Fidei*, at Guaratiba. Is the Lord not telling us, perhaps, that we ourselves are the true field of faith, the true *Campus Fidei*, and that it is not some geographical location? Yes, it is true—each one of us, each one of you, me, everyone! To be missionary disciples means to know that we are the field of faith of God! Starting with the name of the place where we are, *Campus Fidei*, the field of faith, I have thought of three images that can help us better understand what it means to be a disciple and a missionary. First, a field is a place for sowing seeds; second, a field is a training ground; and third, a field is a construction site.

1. *First: A field is a place for sowing seeds.* We all know the parable where Jesus speaks of a sower who went out to sow seeds in the field; some seed fell on the path, some on rocky ground, some among thorns, where it could not grow; other seed fell on good soil and brought forth much fruit (cf. Mt 13:1–9). Jesus himself explains the meaning of the parable: the seed is the word of God sown in our hearts (cf. Mt 13:18–23). Today... every day, but today in a particular way, Jesus is sowing the seed. When we accept the word of God, then we are the field of faith! Please, let Christ and his word enter your life; let the seed of the word of God enter, let it blossom, and let it grow. God will take care of everything, but let him work in you and bring about this growth.

Jesus tells us that the seed that fell on the path or on the rocky ground or among the thorns bore no fruit. I believe that we can ask ourselves honestly: What kind of ground are we? What kind of ground do we want to be? Maybe sometimes we are like the path: we hear the Lord's word but it changes nothing in our lives because we let ourselves be numbed by all the superficial voices competing for our attention. I ask you, but do not respond immediately; respond in your own heart: Am I a young person who is numb? Or perhaps we are like the rocky ground: we receive Jesus with enthusiasm, but we falter and, when faced with difficulties, we don't have the courage to swim against the tide. Again, respond in your heart: am I courageous or am I a coward? Or maybe we are like the thorny ground: negativity and negative feelings choke the Lord's word in us (cf. Mt 13:18–22). Respond once more in your heart: Do I have the habit of playing both sides of the fence, making a good impression on both God and the devil? Do I want to receive the seed from Jesus and at the same time water the thorns and the weeds that grow in my heart? But [here,] today, I am sure that the seed is able to fall on good soil. We are listening to these witnesses, telling of how the seed has fallen on good soil. "No, Father, I am not good soil; I am a disaster, and I am full of stones, of thorns, of everything." Yes, maybe this is so on the surface, but free a little piece, a small piece of good soil, and let the seed fall there and watch as it grows. I know that you want to be good soil, true Christians, authentic Christians, not part-time Christians: "starchy," aloof, and Christian in "appearance only." I know that you don't want to be duped by a false freedom, always at the beck and call of momentary fashions and fads. I know that you are aiming high, at long-lasting decisions that are meaningful. Is that true, or am I wrong? Am I right? Good; if it is true, let's do this: in silence, let us all look into our hearts and then tell Jesus that we want to receive the seed of his Word. Say to him: "Jesus, look upon the stones, the thorns, and the weeds that I have, but look also upon this small piece of ground that I offer to you so that the seed may enter my heart." In silence, let us allow the seed of Jesus to enter our hearts. Remember this moment. Everyone knows the seed that has been received. Allow it to grow, and God will nurture it.

2. *Second: Beyond being a place of sowing, the field is a training ground.* Jesus asks us to follow him for life, he asks us to be his disciples, to "play on his team." Most of you love sports! Here in Brazil, as in other countries, football is a national passion. Right? Now, what do players do when they are asked to join a team? They have to train, and to train a lot! The same is true of our lives as the Lord's disciples. Saint Paul, describing Christians, tells us: "Athletes deny themselves all sorts of things; they do this to win a crown of leaves that withers, but we a crown that is imperishable" (1 Cor 9:25). Jesus offers us something bigger than the World Cup! Something bigger than the World Cup! Jesus offers us the possibility of a fruitful life, a life of happiness; he also offers us a future with him, an endless future, in eternal life. That is what Jesus offers us. But he asks us to pay admission, and the cost of admission is that we train ourselves "to get in shape," so that we can face every situation in life undaunted, bearing witness to our faith by talking with him in prayer. Father, are you asking us all to pray? I ask you all...but reply in the silence of your heart, not aloud: Do I pray? Do I speak with Jesus, or am I frightened of silence? Do I allow the Holy Spirit to speak in my heart? Do I ask Jesus: What do you want me to do, what do you want from my life? This is training. Ask Jesus, speak to Jesus, and if

you make a mistake in your life, if you should fall, if you should do something wrong, don't be afraid. "Jesus, look at what I have done, what must I now do?" Speak continually with Jesus, in the good times and in the bad, when you do right and when you do wrong. Do not fear him! This is prayer. And through this, you train yourselves in dialogue with Jesus on this path of being missionary disciples. By the sacraments, which make his life grow within us and conform us to Christ; by loving one another, learning to listen, to understand, to forgive, to be accepting, and to help others, everybody, with no one excluded or ostracized. Dear young people, be true "athletes for Christ"!

3. *And third: A field is a construction site.* We are seeing this happen before us with our own eyes: young people have engaged in and given themselves to the work of building up the Church. When our heart is good soil that receives the word of God, when "we build up a sweat" in trying to live as Christians, we experience something tremendous: we are never alone, we are part of a family of brothers and sisters, all journeying on the same path; we are part of the Church. These young people have not been working alone; together they are creating a path and building up the Church; together they have done what Saint Francis did—build up and repair the Church. I ask you: Do you want to build up the Church?

[*Yes!*]

Are you encouraged to do so?

[*Yes!*]

And tomorrow, will you have forgotten the "yes" you have spoken today?

[*No!*]

That makes me happy! We are part of the Church, indeed, we are building up the Church and we are making history. Young people, please, don't put yourselves at the tail-end of history. Be active members! Go on the offensive! Play down the field, build a better world, a world of brothers and sisters, a world of justice, of love, of peace, of fraternity, of solidarity. Play always on the offensive!

Saint Peter tells us that we are living stones, which form a spiritual edifice (cf. 1 Pet 2:5). As we look at this platform, we see that it is in the shape of a church, built up with living stones. In the Church of Jesus, we ourselves are the living stones. Jesus is asking us to build up his Church; each one of us is a living stone, a small part of the edifice; when the rain comes, if a piece is missing, there is a leak and water comes in. Don't build a little chapel that holds only a small group of persons. Jesus asks us to make his living Church so large that it can hold all of humanity, that it can be a home for everyone! To me, to you, to each of us he says: "Go and make disciples of all nations." Tonight, let us answer him: "Yes, Lord, I too want to be a living stone; together we want to build up the Church of Jesus! I want to go forth and build up the Church of Christ!" Are you eager to make this happen again? I want to go out and build up the Church of Christ, let us say this together...

[*The young people repeat,*
"I want to go out and build up the Church of Christ!"]

You must always remember that you have said this together.

Your young hearts want to build a better world. I have been closely following the news reports of the many young people who throughout the world have taken to the streets in order to express their desire for a more just and fraternal society. Young people in the streets. It is the young who want to be the protagonists of change. Please, don't leave it to others to be the protagonists of change. You are the ones who hold the future! You... Through you the future is fulfilled in the world. I ask you also to be protagonists of transformation. Continue to overcome apathy, offering a Christian response to the social and political anxieties that are arising in various parts of the world. I ask you to be builders of the world, to work for a better world. Dear young people, please, don't be observers of life, but get involved. Jesus did not remain an observer, but he immersed himself. Don't be observers, but immerse yourselves in the reality of life, as Jesus did.

One question remains: Where do we start? Whom do we ask to begin this work? Some people once asked Mother Teresa of Calcutta what needed to change in the Church, and which wall should they start with. They asked her, where is the starting point? And she replied, you and I are the starting point! This woman showed determination! She knew where to start. And today I make her words my own and I say to you: Shall we begin? Where? With you and me! Each one of you, once again in silence, ask yourself: If I must begin with myself, where exactly do I start? Each one of you, open your heart, so that Jesus may tell you where to start.

Dear friends, never forget that you are the field of faith! You are Christ's athletes! You are called to build a more beautiful Church and a better world. Let us lift our gaze to Our Lady. Mary helps us to follow Jesus. She gives us the example by her own "yes" to God: "I am the servant of the Lord; let it be done to me as you say" (Lk 1:38). All together, let us join Mary in saying to God: Let it be done to me as you say. Amen!

Swimming against the Tide

With Volunteers of the Twenty-eighth World Youth Day
Pavilion 5 of the Rio Center, Rio de Janeiro
July 28, 2013

Dear Volunteers,

Good evening! I could not return to Rome without first thanking all of you in a personal and affectionate way for the work and dedication with which you have accompanied, helped, and served the thousands of young pilgrims, and for the countless little ways by which you have made this World Youth Day an unforgettable experience of faith. With your smiles, your acts of kindness, and your willingness to serve, you have shown that "it is more blessed to give than to receive" (Acts 20:35).

The service you have provided during these days brings to mind the mission of Saint John the Baptist, who prepared the way for Jesus. Every one of you, each in his or her own way, was instrumental in enabling thousands of young people to "prepare the way" to meet Jesus. And this is the most beautiful service we can give as missionary disciples. To prepare the way so that all people may know, meet, and love the Lord. To you who in these days responded with such readiness and generosity to the call to be volunteers for World Youth Day, I say: May you always be generous with God and with others: one loses nothing thereby, but gains great enrichment in life.

God calls you to make definitive choices, and he has a plan for each of you: to discover that plan and to respond to your vocation is to move toward personal fulfillment. God calls each of us to be holy... but he has a particular path for each one of us. Some are called to holiness through family life in the sacrament of marriage. Today, there are those who say that marriage is out of fashion. Is it out of fashion? In a culture of relativism and the ephemeral, many preach the importance of "enjoying" the moment. They say that it is not worth making a life-long commitment, making a definitive decision, "forever," because we do not know what tomorrow will bring. I ask you, instead, to be revolutionaries. I ask you to swim against the tide. Yes, I am asking you to rebel against this culture that sees everything as temporary and that ultimately believes you are incapable of responsibility, that believes you are incapable of true love. I have confidence in you and I pray for you. Have the courage "to swim against the tide." And also have the courage to be happy.

The Lord calls some to be priests, to give themselves to him more fully, so as to love all people with the heart of the Good Shepherd. Some he calls to the service of others in the religious life, devoting themselves in monasteries to praying for the good of the world, and in various areas of the apostolate, giving of themselves for the sake of all, especially those most in need. I will never forget that 21st of September—I was seventeen years old—when, after stopping in at the

Church of San José de Flores to go to confession, I first heard God calling me. Do not be afraid of what God asks of you! It is worth saying "yes" to God. In him we find joy!

Dear young people, some of you may not yet know what you will do with your lives. Ask the Lord, and he will show you the way. The young Samuel kept hearing the voice of the Lord who was calling him, but he did not understand or know what to say, yet with the help of the priest Eli, in the end he answered: Speak, Lord, for I am listening (cf. 1 Sam 3:1–10). You too can ask the Lord: What do you want me to do? What path am I to follow?

The Adventure of Mercy

Welcoming Ceremony, Jordan Park, Błonia, Kraków
July 28, 2016

Dear Young Friends,

Good evening! In this, the land of his birth, I especially want to thank Saint John Paul II [*loud applause*]—louder, louder!—who first came up with the idea of these meetings and gave them such momentum. From his place in heaven, he is with us and he sees all of you: so many young people from such a variety of nations, cultures, and languages but with one aim, that of celebrating Jesus who is living in our midst. Do you understand this? To celebrate Jesus who is living in our midst! To say that Jesus is alive means to rekindle our enthusiasm for following him, to renew our passionate desire to be his disciples. What better opportunity to renew our friendship with Jesus than by building friendships among yourselves! What better way to build our friendship with Jesus than by sharing him with others! What better way to experience the contagious joy of the Gospel than by striving to bring the Good News to all kinds of painful and difficult situations!

And it is Jesus who has called us to this thirty-first World Youth Day. Jesus tells us: "Blessed are the merciful, for they shall find mercy" (Mt 5:7). Blessed indeed are they who can forgive, who show heartfelt compassion, who are capable of offering the very best to others; the best, not what is left over: the best!

In my years as a bishop, I have learned one thing—well, I have learned many, but I want to share one with you now: nothing is more beautiful than seeing the enthusiasm, dedication, zeal, and energy with which so many young people live their lives. This is beautiful! And where does this beauty come from? When Jesus touches a young person's heart, he or she becomes capable of truly great things. It is exciting to listen to you share your dreams, your questions, and your impatience with those who say that things cannot change—those whom I call "quietists," who say that nothing can change. No! Young people have the strength to challenge them! But...maybe some are not so sure about this...I ask you, and you respond: Can things change?

[*Yes!*]

I cannot hear you!

[*Yes!*]

That's good. For me, it is a gift of God to see so many of you, with all your questions, trying to make a difference. It is beautiful and heart-warming to see all that restlessness! Today the Church looks to you, and, I would add, the world looks to you, and wants to learn from you, to be reassured that the Father's mercy has an ever-youthful face, and constantly invites us to be part of his kingdom. It is a kingdom of joy, a kingdom always joyful, always driving us forward, a kingdom able to give us the strength to change things. I have forgotten and so I repeat my question to you: Can things change?

[*Yes!*]

Agreed.

Knowing your enthusiasm for mission, I repeat: mercy always has a youthful face! A merciful heart is motivated to move beyond its comfort zone. A merciful heart can go out and meet others; it is ready to embrace everyone. A merciful heart is able to be a place of refuge for those who are without a home or have lost their home; it is able to build a home and a family for those forced to emigrate; it knows the meaning of tenderness and compassion. A merciful heart can share its bread with the hungry and welcome refugees and migrants. To say the word "mercy" along with you is to speak of opportunity, future, commitment, trust, openness, hospitality, compassion, and dreams. But are you able to dream?

[*Yes!*]

When the heart is open and able to dream, there is room for mercy, there is room to caress those who suffer, there is room to draw close to those who have no peace of heart or who do not have the bare necessities to live, or to those who do not have the most beautiful thing of all: the faith. Mercy. Let us together repeat this word: mercy. All of you!

[*Mercy!*]

Again!

[*Mercy!*]

And once more, so the whole world can hear you!

[*Mercy!*]

Let me tell you another thing I have learned over these years. I do not want to offend anyone, but it pains me to meet young people who seem to have opted for "early retirement." This pains me. Young people who seem to retire at twenty-three, twenty-four, twenty-five years of age. This pains me. I worry when I see young people who have "thrown in the towel" before the game has even begun, who are defeated even before they begin to play. I am saddened to see young people who walk around glumly as if life had no meaning. Deep down, young people like this are bored . . . and boring; they bore others, and this upsets me. But it is also hard, and troubling, to see young people who waste their lives looking for thrills or a feeling of being alive by taking dark paths and in the end having to pay . . . and pay dearly. Think of so many young people you know who have chosen this path. It is disturbing to see young people squandering some of the best years of their lives, wasting their energy by running after peddlers of false illusions, and they do exist, (where I come from, we call them "vendors of smoke"), who rob you of what is best in you. This pains me. I am sure that among you there are no such persons, but I want to tell you: there are young people who have gone into retirement, who have thrown in the towel before the game has even begun; there are young people who are enthralled by false illusions and end up in nothingness.

We are gathered here to help one another, because we do not want to be robbed of the best of ourselves. We don't want to be robbed of our energy, our joy, our dreams by false hopes.

So I ask you: Are you looking for empty thrills in life, or do you want to feel a power that can give you a lasting sense of life and fulfillment? Empty thrills or the power of grace? What do you want: deadening thrills or the power of fullness? What do you want?

[The power of fullness!]

I cannot hear you very well.

[The power of fullness!]

To find fulfillment, to gain new life, there is a way, a way that is not for sale, that cannot be purchased, a way that is not a thing or an object, but a person. His name is Jesus Christ. I ask you: Can you buy Jesus Christ?

[No!]

Can Jesus Christ be bought at a shop?

[No!]

Jesus Christ is a gift, a gift from the Father, the gift from our Father. Who is Jesus Christ? All together! Jesus Christ is a gift! All together!

[He is a gift!]

He is the Father's gift.

Jesus can give you true passion for life. Jesus inspires us not to settle for less, but to give the very best of ourselves. Jesus challenges us, spurs us on, and helps us keep trying whenever we are tempted to give up. Jesus pushes us to keep our sights high and to dream of great things. You might say to me, "But Father, it is so difficult to dream of great things, it is so difficult to rise up, to be always moving forward and upward. Father, I am weak, I fall, and I try but so many times I fall down." Mountaineers, as they climb mountains, sing a very beautiful song the words of which go like this: "In the art of climbing, it is not important that you do not fall down, but that you do not stay down." If you are weak, if you fall, look up a little, for there is Jesus' hand extended to you as he says: "Rise up, come with me." "And what if I fall again?" Rise again. "And what if I fall yet again?" Rise yet again. Peter once asked the Lord: "Lord, how many times?" And the reply came: "seventy times seven." The hand of Jesus is always extended, ready to lift us up again when we fall. Do you understand?

[*Yes!*]

In the Gospel, we heard how Jesus, on his way to Jerusalem, stopped at a home—the home of Martha, Mary, and Lazarus—and was welcomed. He stopped, went in, and spent time with them. The two women welcomed him because they knew he was open and attentive. Our many jobs and responsibilities can make us a bit like Martha: busy, scattered, constantly running from place to place... but we can also be like Mary: whenever we see a beautiful landscape, or look at a video from a friend on our mobile phone, we can stop and think, stop and listen... In our own day, Jesus wants to stop and enter our home—your home, my home—enter into our hearts. Jesus will look at us hurrying about with all our concerns, as he did with Martha... and he will wait for us to listen to him, like Mary, to make space for him amid the bustle. May these be days given over to Jesus and to listening to one another. May they help us welcome Jesus in all those with whom we share our homes, our neighborhoods, our groups, and our schools.

Whoever welcomes Jesus learns to love as Jesus does. So he asks us if we want a full life. And, in his name, I ask you: Do you want a full life? Start right this moment by letting yourself be open and attentive! Because happiness is sown and blossoms in mercy. That is his answer, his offer, his challenge, his adventure: mercy. Mercy always has a youthful face. Like that of Mary of Bethany, who sat as a disciple at the feet of Jesus and joyfully listened to his words, since she knew that there she would find peace. Like that of Mary of Nazareth, whose daring "yes" launched her on the adventure of mercy. All generations would call her blessed; to all of us she is the "Mother of Mercy." Let us call upon her together: Mary, Mother of Mercy.

All together, let us ask the Lord, each repeating in the silence of his or her heart: "Lord, launch us on the adventure of mercy! Launch us on the adventure of building bridges and tearing down walls, be they barriers or barbed wire. Launch us on the adventure of helping the poor, those who feel lonely and abandoned, or who no longer find meaning in their lives. Launch us on the journey of accompanying those who do not know you, and telling them carefully and respectfully your Name, the reason for our faith. Send us, like Mary of Bethany, to listen attentively to those we do not understand, those of other cultures and peoples, even those we are afraid of because we consider them a threat. Make us attentive to our elders, to our grandparents, as Mary of Nazareth was to Elizabeth, in order to learn from their wisdom. I ask you: Do you speak to your grandparents?

[*Yes!*]

That is good! Seek your grandparents. They have the wisdom of life and can tell you things that will stir your hearts.

The Way of Hope

Way of the Cross with Young People
Jordan Park in Błonia, Kraków, July 29, 2016

I was hungry and you gave me food,
I was thirsty and you gave me something to drink,
I was a stranger and you welcomed me,
I was naked and you gave me clothing,
I was sick and you took care of me,
I was in prison and you visited me. (Mt 25:35–36)

These words of Jesus answer the question that arises so often in our minds and hearts: "Where is God?" Where is God, if evil is present in our world, if there are men and women who are hungry and thirsty, homeless, exiles, and refugees? Where is God, when innocent persons die as a result of violence, terrorism, and war? Where is God, when cruel diseases break the bonds of life and affection? Or when children are exploited and demeaned, and they too suffer from grave illness? Where is God, amid the anguish of those who doubt and are troubled in spirit? These are questions that humanly speaking have no answer. We can only look to Jesus and ask him. And Jesus' answer is this:

"God is in them." Jesus is in them; he suffers in them and deeply identifies with each of them. He is so closely united to them as to form with them, as it were, "one body."

Jesus himself chose to identify with these our brothers and sisters enduring pain and anguish by agreeing to tread the "way of sorrows" that led to Calvary. By dying on the cross, he surrendered himself into the hands of the Father, taking upon himself and in himself, with self-sacrificing love, the physical, moral, and spiritual wounds of all humanity. By embracing the wood of the cross, Jesus embraced the nakedness, the hunger and thirst, the loneliness, the pain and death of men and women of all times. Tonight Jesus, and we with him, embrace with particular love our brothers and sisters from Syria who have fled from the war. We greet them and we welcome them with fraternal affection and friendship.

By following Jesus along the Way of the Cross, we have once again realized the importance of imitating him through the fourteen *works of mercy*. These help us to be open to God's mercy, to implore the grace to appreciate that without mercy we can do nothing; without mercy, neither I nor you nor any of us can do a thing. Let us first consider the seven corporal works of mercy: feeding the hungry, giving drink to the thirsty, clothing the naked, sheltering the homeless, visiting the sick and those in prison, and burying the dead. Freely we have received, so freely let us give. We are called to serve the crucified Jesus in all those who are marginalized, to touch his sacred flesh in those who are disadvantaged, in those who hunger and thirst, in the naked and imprisoned, the sick and unemployed, in those who are persecuted, refugees and migrants. There we find our God;

there we touch the Lord. Jesus himself told us this when he explained the criterion on which we will be judged: whenever we do these things to the least of our brothers and sisters, we do them to him (cf. Mt 25:31–46).

After the corporal works of mercy come the spiritual works: counseling the doubtful, instructing the ignorant, admonishing sinners, consoling the afflicted, pardoning offences, bearing wrongs patiently, praying for the living and the dead. In welcoming the outcast who suffers physically and in welcoming sinners who suffer spiritually, our credibility as Christians is at stake...Not in ideas, but in our actions.

Humanity today needs men and women, and especially young people like yourselves, who do not wish to live their lives "halfway," young people ready to spend their lives freely in service to those of their brothers and sisters who are poorest and most vulnerable, in imitation of Christ who gave himself completely for our salvation. In the face of evil, suffering, and sin, the only response possible for a disciple of Jesus is the gift of self, even of one's own life, in imitation of Christ; it is the attitude of service. Unless those who call themselves Christians live to serve, their lives are not worth living; by their lives, they deny Jesus Christ.

This evening, dear friends, the Lord once more asks you to be in the forefront of serving others. He wants to make of you *a concrete response* to the needs and sufferings of humanity. He wants you to be signs of his merciful love for our time! To enable you to carry out this mission, he shows you the way of personal commitment and self-sacrifice. It is the Way of the Cross. The Way of the Cross is the way of fidelity in following Jesus to the end, in the often dramatic situations of everyday life. It is a way that does not fear lack of success, ostracism, or solitude, because it fills ours hearts with the fullness of Jesus. The Way of the Cross is the way of God's own life, his "style," which Jesus brings even to the pathways of a society at times divided, unjust, and corrupt.

The Way of the Cross is not an exercise in sadomasochism; the Way of the Cross alone defeats sin, evil, and death, for it leads to the radiant light of Christ's resurrection and opens the horizons of a new and fuller life. It is the way of hope, the way of the future. Those who take up this way with generosity and faith give hope to the future and to humanity. Those who take up this way with generosity and faith sow seeds of hope. I want you to be sowers of hope.

Dear young people, on that Good Friday many disciples went back crestfallen to their homes. Others chose to go out to the country to forget the cross. I ask you: but I want each of you to answer in silence in the depths of your heart. How do you want to go back this evening to your own homes, to the places where you are staying, to your tents? How do you want to go back this evening to be alone with your thoughts? The world is watching us. It's up to each of you to answer the challenge that this question sets before you.

Building Bridges

Prayer Vigil with Young People
Campus Misericordiae, Kraków, July 30, 2016

Dear Young Friends,

Good evening! We have come here from different parts of the world, from different continents, countries, languages, cultures and peoples. Some of us are sons and daughters of nations that may be at odds and engaged in various conflicts or even open war. Others of us come from countries that may be at "peace," free of war and conflict, where most of the terrible things occurring in our world are simply a story on the evening news. But think about it. For us here, today, coming from different parts of the world, the suffering and the wars that many young people experience are no longer anonymous, something we read about in the papers. They have a name, they have a face, they have a story, they are close at hand. Today the war in Syria has caused pain and suffering for so many people, for so many young people like our brave friend Rand, who has come here and asked us to pray for her beloved country.

Some situations seem distant until in some way we touch them. We don't appreciate certain things because we see them only on the screen of a cell phone or a computer. But when we come into contact with life, with people's lives, not just images on a screen, something powerful happens. We all feel the need to get involved. To see that there are no more "forgotten cities," to use Rand's words, or brothers and sisters of ours "surrounded by death and killing," completely helpless.

Dear friends, I ask that we join in prayer for the sufferings of all the victims of war, of this war today in the world. Once and for all, may we realize that nothing justifies shedding the blood of a brother or sister; that nothing is more precious than the person next to us. In asking you to pray for this, I would also like to thank Natalia and Miguel for sharing their own battles and inner conflicts. You told us about your struggles, and about how you succeeded in overcoming them. Both of you are a living sign of what God's mercy wants to accomplish in us.

This is no time for denouncing anyone. We don't want to fight, or tear down, or insult anyone. We have no desire to conquer hatred with more hatred, violence with more violence, terror with more terror. We are here today because the Lord has called us together. Our response to a world at war has a name: its name is fraternity, its name is brotherhood, its name is communion, its name is family. We celebrate the fact that we come from different cultures, that we come together to pray. Let our best word, our best argument, be our unity in prayer. Let us take a moment of silence and pray. Let us place before the Lord these testimonies of our friends, and let us identify with those for whom "the family is a meaningless concept, the home only a place to sleep and eat," and with those who live in fear that their mistakes and sins have made them outcasts. Let us also place before the Lord your own "battles," our "battles," the interior struggles that each one of us carries in his or her heart. And so, to live as a family, in fraternity, I invite all of you together to stand, to take each other's hand, and to pray in silence. All of us.

[*SILENCE*]

As we were praying, I thought of the apostles on the day of Pentecost. Picturing them can help us come to appreciate all that God dreams of accomplishing in our lives, in us and with us. That day, the disciples were together in fear behind locked doors. They felt threatened, surrounded by an atmosphere of persecution that had cornered them in a little room and left them silent and paralyzed. Fear had taken hold of them. Then, in that situation, something spectacular, something astonishing, occurred. The Holy Spirit and tongues as of fire came to rest upon each of them, propelling them toward an undreamt-of adventure. It brought about a total change!

We have heard three testimonies. Our hearts were touched by these young people's stories, by their lives. We have seen how, like the disciples, they experienced similar moments, living through times of great fear, when it seemed like everything was falling apart. The fear and anguish born of knowing that leaving home might mean never again seeing their loved ones, the fear of not feeling appreciated or loved, the fear of having no choices. They shared with us the same experience the disciples had; they felt the kind of fear that leads to only one thing. Where does fear lead us? To the feeling of being closed in on oneself, trapped. Once we feel that way, our fear starts to fester and is inevitably joined by its "twin sister," paralysis: the feeling of being paralyzed. Thinking that in this world, in our cities and in our communities, there is no longer any room to grow, to dream, to create, to gaze at new horizons—in a word, to live—is one of the worst things that can happen to us in life, and especially at a young age. When we are paralyzed, we miss the magic of encountering others, making friends, sharing dreams, walking side-by-side of others. Paralysis distances us from others; it prevents us from taking each other's hand, and locks us in.

But in life there is another, even more dangerous, kind of paralysis. It is not easy to put our finger on it. I like to describe it as the paralysis that comes from confusing happiness with a sofa. In other words, to think that in order to be happy all we need is a good sofa. A sofa that makes us feel comfortable, calm, safe. A sofa like one of those we have nowadays with a built-in massage unit to put us to sleep. A sofa that promises us hours of comfort so we can escape to the world of videogames and spend hours in front of a computer screen. A sofa that keeps us safe from any kind of pain and fear. A sofa that allows us to stay home without needing to work at, or worry about, anything. "Sofa-happiness"! That is probably the most harmful and insidious form of paralysis, the one that can cause the greatest harm to young people. And why does this happen, Father? Because, little by little, without even realizing it, we start to nod off, to grow drowsy and dull.

The other day, I spoke about young people who go into retirement at the age of twenty; today I speak about young persons who nod off, grow drowsy and dull, while others—

perhaps more alert than we are, but not necessarily better—decide our future for us. For many people, in fact, it is much easier and better to have drowsy and dull kids who confuse happiness with a sofa. For many people, that is more convenient than having young people who are alert and searching, trying to respond to God's dream and to all the restlessness present in the human heart. I ask you: Do you want to be young people who nod off, who are drowsy and dull?

[*No!*]

Do you want others to decide your future for you?

[*No!*]

Do you want to be free?

[*Yes!*]

Do you want to be alert?

[*Yes!*]

Do you want to work hard for your future?

[*Yes!*]

You don't seem very convinced... Do you want to work hard for your future?

[*Yes!*]

...Dear young people, we didn't come into this work to "vegetate," to take it easy, to make our lives a comfortable sofa to fall asleep on. No, we came for another reason: to leave a mark. It is very sad to pass through life without leaving a mark. But when we opt for ease and convenience, for confusing happiness with consumption, then we end up paying a high price indeed: we lose our freedom. We are not free to leave a mark. We lose our freedom. This is the high price we pay. There are so many people who do not want the young to be free; there are so many people who do not wish you well, who want you to be drowsy and dull, and never free! No, this must not be so! We must defend our freedom!

This is itself a great form of paralysis, whenever we start thinking that happiness is the same as comfort and convenience, that being happy means going through life asleep or on tranquilizers, that the only way to be happy is to live in a haze. Certainly, drugs are bad, but there are plenty of other socially acceptable drugs that can end up enslaving us just much. One way or another, they rob us of our greatest treasure: our freedom. They strip us of our freedom.

My friends, Jesus is the Lord of risk, he is the Lord of the eternal "more." Jesus is not the Lord of comfort, security, and ease. Following Jesus demands a good dose of courage, a readiness to trade in the sofa for a pair of walking shoes and to set out on new and uncharted paths. To blaze trails that open up new horizons capable of spreading joy, the joy that is born of God's love and wells up in your hearts with every act of mercy. To take the path of the "craziness" of our God, who teaches us to encounter him in the hungry, the thirsty, the naked, the sick, the friend in trouble, the prisoner, the refugee, the migrant, and our neighbors who feel abandoned. To take the path of our God, who encourages us to be politicians, thinkers, social activists. The God who encourages us to devise an economy marked by greater solidarity than our own. In all the settings in which you find yourselves, God's love invites you to bring the Good News, making of your own lives a gift to him and to others. This means being courageous, this means being free!

You might say to me: Father, that is not for everybody, but just for a chosen few. True, and those chosen are all who are ready to share their lives with others. Just as the Holy Spirit transformed the hearts of the disciples on the day of Pentecost, when they had been paralyzed, so he did with our friends who shared their testimonies.

That is the secret, dear friends, and all of us are called to share in it. God expects something from you. Have you understood this? God expects something from you, God wants something from you. God hopes in you. God comes to break down all our fences, to open the doors of our lives, our dreams, our ways of seeing things. God comes to break open everything that keeps you closed in. He is encouraging you to dream. He wants to make you see that, with you, the world can be different. For the fact is that, unless you offer the best of yourselves, the world will never be different. This is the challenge.

The times we live in do not call for young "couch potatoes," but for young people with shoes, or better, laced boots. The times we live in require only active players on the field, and there is no room for those who sit on the bench. Today's world demands that you be a protagonist of history, because life is always beautiful when we choose to live it fully, when we choose to leave a mark. History today calls us to defend our dignity and not to let others decide our future. No! We must decide our future, you must decide your future! As he did on Pentecost, the Lord wants to work one of the greatest miracles we can experience; he wants to turn your hands, my hands, our hands, into signs of reconciliation, of communion, of creation. He wants your hands to continue building the world of today. And he wants to build that world with you. And what is your response? Yes or no?

[*Yes!*]

You might say to me: Father, but I have my limits, I am a sinner, what can I do? When the Lord calls us, he doesn't worry about what we are, what we have been, or what we have done or not done. Quite the opposite. When he calls us, he is thinking about everything we have to give, all the love we are capable of spreading. His bets are on the future, on tomorrow. Jesus is pointing you to the future, and never to the museum.

So today, my friends, Jesus is inviting you, calling you, to leave your mark on life, to leave a mark on history, your own and that of many others as well.

Life nowadays tells us that it is much easier to concentrate on what divides us, what keeps us apart. People try to make us believe that being closed in on ourselves is the best way to safeguard ourselves from harm. Today, we adults need you to teach us, as you are doing today, how to live in diversity, in dialogue, to experience multiculturalism not as a threat but an opportunity. You are an opportunity for the future. Have the courage to teach us, have the courage to show us that it is easier to build bridges than walls! We need to learn this. Together we ask that you challenge us to take the path of fraternity. May you point the finger at us, if we choose the path of walls, the path of enmity, the path of war. To build bridges...

Do you know which is the first bridge that has to be built? It is a bridge that we can build here and now—by reaching out and taking each other's hand. Come, build it now. Build this human bridge, take each other's hand, all of you: it is the first of bridges, it is the human bridge, it is the first, it is the model. There is always a risk, as I said the other day, of offering your hand and having no one take it. But in life we need to take a risk, for the person who does not take a risk never wins. With this bridge we can move forward. Here, this is the primordial bridge: take each other's hand. Thank you. This is a great bridge of brother-hood, and would that the powers of this world might learn to build it...not for pictures and ulterior motives, but for building ever bigger bridges. May this human bridge be the beginning of many, many others; in that way, it will leave a mark.

Today Jesus, who is the way, the truth, and the life, is calling you, you, and you to leave your mark on history. He who is life is asking each of you to leave a mark that brings life to your own history and that of many others. He who is truth is asking you to abandon the paths of rejection, divi-sion, and emptiness. Are you up to this?

[*Yes!*]

Are you up to this?

[*Yes!*]

What answer will you give—and I'd like to see it—with your hands and with your feet, to the Lord, who is the way, the truth, and the life? Are you up to this?

[*Yes!*]

May the Lord bless your dreams. Thank you!

Never Stop Moving Ahead

Prayer Vigil in Preparation for World Youth Day
Papal Basilica of Saint Mary Major, Rome, April 8, 2017

Dear Young Friends,

Thank you for coming! This evening marks a double beginning. It is the beginning of the journey toward the Synod, which has a very long name—"Young People, the Faith, and Vocational Discernment," but we can just call it the Synod of Young People. That way it is easier to understand! It is also a second beginning, the beginning of our journey to Panama. The Archbishop of Panama is with us, and I greet him warmly.

We have listened to the Gospel, prayed, sung, and brought flowers to the Madonna, our Mother. We also brought the World Youth Day cross, which has come from Kraków and will be handed over tomorrow to the young people from Panama. From Kraków to Panama, with the synod in between. A synod from which no young person should feel excluded!

Some people say: "Let's hold the synod for young Catholics, for those belonging to Catholic groups; that way it will be better." No! The synod is meant to be the synod *for* and *of* all young people. Young people are its protagonists "But even young people who consider themselves agnostics?" Yes! "Even young people whose faith is lukewarm?" Yes! "Even young people who no longer go to Church?" Yes! "Even young people who—I don't know if there are any here, maybe one or two—consider themselves atheists?" Yes! This is the Synod of young people and we want to *listen to one another*. Every young person has something to say to others. He or she has something to say to adults, something to say to priests, sisters, bishops, and even the pope. All of us need to listen to you!

Let's think back to Kraków; the cross is a reminder. There I said two things. Perhaps some of you may remember. First, it is not good to see a young person already retired at the age of twenty! Second, it is also not good to see a young person spending his or her life on a couch. Isn't this the truth? We need *young people who are neither retired nor couch potatoes!* We need young people who are on the road and moving forward, at each other's side but looking ahead to the future!

In the Gospel (cf. Lk 1:39–45) we heard how Mary receives that grace, that immense *vocation* of bringing God's gift to us. The Gospel tells us that after hearing that her elderly cousin is expecting a child and needs help, Mary sets out in haste to help her. She hurries! The world today needs young people who "hurry," who don't get tired of hurrying. We need young people who feel a call, who feel that life offers them *a mission*. Young people who, as Maria Lisa (a young religious Sister) said so often in her testimony, are *on the go*. Maria Lisa shared her experience with us: it was an experience of being on the go. We need young people on the go. The world can change only if young people are on the go.

But this is the tragedy of the world today, and of young people today, that *young people are often discarded*. They don't have work, they don't have an ideal to pursue, they lack education, and they lack integration. So many young people have to flee, to migrate to other lands. Young people today, it is painful to say, are often discarded. We cannot tolerate this! We have to hold this synod to say: "We young people are here!" And we are going to Panama to say: "We young people are here, on the march, and we don't want to be discarded! We have something of value to give!"

While Pompeo was talking, I was thinking that twice he was almost at the point of being discarded—when he was eight and again when he was eighteen. But he made it: he was able to pick himself up. Life, when we look up, always surprises us. Maria Lisa said this too. They both said this.

We are on the march, toward the synod and toward Panama. And this march has its risks, but when young people don't take risks, they are already old. We have to take risks.

Maria Lisa said that after receiving the sacrament of confirmation she fell away from the Church. You all know that here in Italy the sacrament of confirmation is called the "sacrament of farewell"! After confirmation, people stop going to church. Why? Because so many young people don't know what to do. But Maria Lisa never stopped, she kept walking: at times along dark ways, poorly lit ways, without ideals or with ideals that she didn't quite understand; but in the end she too made it. As young people, you have to take risks in life. You have to prepare for tomorrow today. The future is in your hands.

In the synod, the entire Church wants to listen to young people: to what they are thinking, to what they want, to what they criticize, and to what they are sorry for. Everything. The Church needs lots more springtime, and springtime is the season of the young.

I want to invite you to make this journey, this march toward the synod and toward Panama, and to make it with joy, with your aspirations, without fear, without shame, and to make it courageously. Courage is needed. But what is also needed is the effort to appreciate the beauty of little things, as Pompeo said: the beauty of everyday life. Be grateful for life, don't ever lose this ability. Be thankful for what you are: "This is how I am, thank you!" So often in life, we waste time asking ourselves: "Who am I?" You can keep asking, "Who am I?" for the rest of your lives. But the real question is: *"For whom* am I?" Like Our Lady, who could ask: *"For whom, for what person, am I"* here and now? She answers, "For my cousin," and off she goes. "For whom am I?"—not "Who am I?" The answer to that second question comes later; it is a question that has to be asked, but first you have to ask *why*: why you do something, something for your entire life, something that makes you *think*, makes you *feel*, makes you *work*. There are these three languages: the language of the *mind*, the language of the *heart*, and the language of the *hands*. Never stop moving ahead.

There is something else I want to tell you. The synod will not be a "chat room." World Youth Day will not be a chat room, or a form of entertainment, or a nice happy experience from which you can then move on. No! *Concrete-*

ness! Life demands concreteness of us. In this liquid culture, we need concreteness, and concreteness is your vocation.

Now I would like to conclude... I had a written speech, but after seeing you, after listening to the testimonies, I thought I should say all the things I just told you. There are going to be times when you don't understand, dark times, painful times, but also wonderful times, times of darkness and times of light... But I want to make one thing clear. We live in the present. At my age, people are getting ready to leave the scene... right? Who can be sure about life? Nobody. At your age, you have the future ahead of you. Life holds out a mission to young people today; the Church holds out a mission, and I would like to entrust you with this mission. It is to go back and talk to your grandparents. Today more than ever we need this bridge, this dialogue, between grandparents and grandchildren, between the young and the elderly. The prophet Joel makes this prophecy: "Your old men shall dream dreams, and your young men shall see visions" (2:28). In other words, the young will make things happen because of their vision. So this is the task I am giving you in the name of the Church. *Talk to older people.* You may say: "But it's boring... They are always talking about the same things..." No! Listen to older people, talk to them, ask them questions. Make them dream, and from those dreams take what you need to move forward, so that you can have a vision and make that vision concrete. This is your mission today. This is the mission the Church gives you today.

Dear young friends, be courageous! You may say: "But Father, I have sinned, I fall so often!" I think of an Alpine song, a lovely song that mountaineers sing: "In the art of scaling a mountain, the important thing is not that you fall; it is that you get up and keep going!" Have you fallen? Get up and keep moving. But think about the dreams your grandfather or grandmother had, make them talk about them, take those things and build the bridge to the future. This is the task and the mission the Church is giving you today.

Thank you so much for your courage and now...off to Panama! I don't know whether I will be there, but the pope will be there! And the pope in Panama will ask you this question: "Did you talk to older people? Did you take the dreams of the elderly and make them visions? Are you making them happen? This is your task. May the Lord bless you. Pray for me, and together let us prepare for the synod and for Panama. Thank you.

.

YOUTH DAY MESSAGES

Message of Pope Francis for the Twenty-ninth World Youth Day, 2014

Blessed are the poor in spirit,
for theirs is the kingdom of heaven. (Mt 5:3)

Dear Young Friends,

How vividly I recall the remarkable meeting we had in Rio de Janeiro for the twenty-eighth World Youth Day. It was a great celebration of faith and fellowship! The wonderful people of Brazil welcomed us with open arms, like the statue of Christ the Redeemer, which looks down from the hill of Corcovado over the magnificent expanse of Copacabana beach. There, on the seashore, Jesus renewed his call to each one of us to become his missionary disciples. May we perceive this call as the most important thing in our lives and share this gift with others, those near and far, even to the distant geographical and existential peripheries of our world.

The next stop on our intercontinental youth pilgrimage will be in Kraków in 2016. As we journey there together over the next three years, I would like to reflect with you on the Beatitudes found in the Gospel of Saint Matthew (5:1–12). This year we will begin by reflecting on the first Beatitude: "Blessed are the poor in spirit, for theirs is the kingdom of heaven" (Mt 5:3). For 2015 I suggest: "Blessed are the pure in heart, for they shall see God" (Mt 5:8). Then, in 2016, our theme will be: "Blessed are the merciful, for they shall obtain mercy" (Mt 5:7).

THE REVOLUTIONARY POWER OF THE BEATITUDES

It is always a joyful experience for us to read and reflect on the beatitudes! Jesus proclaimed them in his first great sermon, preached on the shore of the sea of Galilee. There was a very large crowd, so Jesus went up on the mountain to teach his disciples. That is why it is known as "the Sermon on the Mount." In the Bible, the mountain is regarded as a place where God reveals himself. Jesus, by preaching on the mount, reveals himself to be a divine teacher, a new Moses. What does he tell us? He shows us the way to life, the way that he himself has taken. Jesus himself *is* the way, and he proposes this way as *the path to true happiness*. Throughout his life, from his birth in the stable in Bethlehem until his death on the cross and his resurrection, Jesus embodied the beatitudes. All the promises of God's kingdom were fulfilled in him.

In proclaiming the beatitudes, Jesus asks us to follow him and to travel with him along the path of love, the path that alone leads to eternal life. It is not an easy journey, yet the Lord promises us his grace and he never abandons us. We face so many challenges in life: poverty, distress, humiliation, the struggle for justice, persecutions, the difficulty of daily conversion, the effort to remain faithful to our call to holiness, and many others. But if we open the door to Jesus and allow him to be part of our lives, if we share our joys and sorrows with him, then we will experience the peace and joy that only God, who is infinite love, can give.

The Beatitudes of Jesus are new and revolutionary. They present a model of happiness contrary to what is usually communicated by the media and by prevailing wisdom. A worldly way of thinking finds it scandalous that God became one of us and died on a cross! According to the logic of this world, those whom Jesus proclaimed blessed are regarded as useless, "losers." What is glorified is success at any cost, affluence, the arrogance of power, and self-affirmation at the expense of others.

Jesus challenges us, young friends, to take seriously his approach to life and to decide which path is right for us and leads to true joy. This is the great challenge of faith. Jesus was not afraid to ask his disciples if they truly wanted to follow him or if they preferred to take another path (cf. Jn 6:67). Simon Peter had the courage to reply: "Lord, to whom shall we go? You have the words of eternal life" (Jn 6:68). If you too are able to say "yes" to Jesus, your lives will become both meaningful and fruitful.

THE COURAGE TO BE HAPPY

What does it mean to be "blessed" (*makarioi* in Greek)? To be blessed means to be happy. Tell me: Do you really want to be happy? In an age when we are constantly being enticed by vain and empty illusions of happiness, we risk settling for less and "thinking small" when it comes to the meaning of life. Think big instead! Open your hearts! As Blessed Piergiorgio Frassati once said, "To live without faith, to have no heritage to uphold, to fail to struggle constantly to defend the truth: this is not living. It is scraping by. We should never just scrape by, but really live" (*Letter to I. Bonini*, February 27, 1925). In his homily on the day of Piergiorgio Frassati's beatification (May 20, 1990), John Paul II called him "a man of the Beatitudes" (*AAS 82* [1990], 1518).

If you are really open to the deepest aspirations of your hearts, you will realize that you possess an unquenchable thirst for happiness, and this will allow you to expose and reject the "low cost" offers and approaches all around you. When we look only for success, pleasure, and possessions, and we turn these into idols, we may well have moments of exhilaration, an illusory sense of satisfaction, but ultimately we become enslaved, never satisfied, always looking for more. It is a tragic thing to see a young person who "has everything" but is weary and weak.

Saint John, writing to young people, told them: "You are strong, and the word of God abides in you, and you have overcome the evil one" (1 Jn 2:14). Young people who choose Christ *are* strong: they are fed by his word and they do not need to "stuff themselves" with other things! Have the courage to swim against the tide. Have the courage to be truly happy! Say no to an ephemeral, superficial, and throwaway culture, a culture that assumes you are incapable of taking on responsibility and facing the great challenges of life!

BLESSED ARE THE POOR IN SPIRIT...

The first Beatitude, our theme for the next World Youth Day, says that the *poor in spirit* are blessed, for theirs is the kingdom of heaven. At a time when so many people are suffering as a result of the financial crisis, it might seem strange to link poverty and happiness. How can we consider poverty a blessing?

First of all, let us try to understand what it means to be *"poor in spirit."* When the Son of God became man, he chose the path of poverty and self-emptying. As Saint Paul said in his letter to the Philippians: "Let the same mind be in you that was in Christ Jesus, who, though he was in the form of God, did not count equality with God a thing to be grasped, but emptied himself, taking the form of a servant, being born in human likeness" (2:5–7). Jesus is God who strips himself of his glory. Here we see God's choice to be poor: he was rich and yet he became poor in order to enrich us through his poverty (cf. 2 Cor 8:9). This is the mystery we contemplate in the crib when we see the Son of God lying in a manger, and later on the cross, where his self-emptying reaches its culmination.

The Greek adjective *ptochós* (poor) does not have a purely material meaning. It means "a beggar," and it should be seen as linked to the Jewish notion of the *anawim*, "God's poor." It suggests lowliness, a sense of one's limitations and existential poverty. The *anawim* trust in the Lord, and they know that they can count on him.

As Saint Thérèse of the Child Jesus clearly saw, by his incarnation Jesus came among us as a poor beggar, asking for our love. The *Catechism of the Catholic Church* tells us that "man is a beggar before God" (no. 2559) and that prayer is the encounter of God's thirst and our own thirst (no. 2560).

Saint Francis of Assisi understood perfectly the secret of the Beatitude of the poor in spirit. Indeed, when Jesus spoke to him through the leper and from the crucifix, Francis recognized both God's grandeur and his own lowliness. In his prayer, the Poor Man of Assisi would spend hours asking the Lord: "Who are you?" "Who am I?" He renounced an affluent and carefree life in order to marry "Lady Poverty," to imitate Jesus and to follow the Gospel to the letter. Francis lived *in imitation of Christ in his poverty* and *in love for the poor*—for him the two were inextricably linked, like two sides of one coin.

You might ask me, then: What can we do, specifically, to make *poverty in spirit* a way of life, a real part of our own lives? I will reply by saying three things.

First of all, try to be *free with regard to material things*. The Lord calls us to a Gospel lifestyle marked by temperance, by a refusal to yield to the culture of consumerism. This means being concerned with the essentials and learning to do without all those unneeded extras that hem us in. Let us learn to be detached from possessiveness and from the idolatry of money and lavish spending. Let us put Jesus first. He can free us from the kinds of idol-worship that enslave us. Put your trust in God, dear young friends! He knows and loves us, and he never forgets us. Just as he provides for the lilies of the field (cf. Mt 6:28), so he will make sure that we lack nothing. If we are to come through the financial crisis, we must be also ready to change our lifestyle and avoid wastefulness. Just as we need the courage to be happy, we also need the courage to live simply.

Second, if we are to live by this Beatitude, all of us need to experience *a conversion in the way we see the poor*. We have to care for them and be sensitive to their spiritual and material needs. To you young people I especially entrust the task of restoring solidarity to the heart of human culture. Faced with old and new forms of poverty—unemployment, migration, and addictions of various kinds—we have the duty to be alert and thoughtful, avoiding the temptation to remain indifferent. We have to remember all those who feel unloved, who have no hope for the future and who have given up on life out of discouragement, disappointment, or fear. We have to learn to be on the side of the poor, and not just indulge in rhetoric about the poor! Let us go out to meet them, look into their eyes and listen to them. The poor provide us with a concrete opportunity to encounter Christ himself, and to touch his suffering flesh.

However—and this is my third point—the poor are not just people to whom we can give something. They have *much to offer us and to teach us*. How much we have to learn from the wisdom of the poor! Think about it: several hundred years ago a saint, Benedict Joseph Labré, who lived on the streets of Rome from the alms he received, became a spiritual guide to all sorts of people, including nobles and prelates. In a very real way, the poor are our teachers. They show us that people's value is not measured by their possessions or how much money they have in the bank. A poor person, a person lacking material possessions, always maintains his or her dignity. The poor can teach us much about humility and trust in God. In the parable of the Pharisee and the tax collector (cf. Lk 18:9–14), Jesus holds the tax collector up as a model because of his humility and his acknowledgment that he is a sinner. The widow who gave her last two coins to the temple treasury is an example of the generosity of all those who have next to nothing and yet give away everything they have (Lk 21:1–4).

... FOR THEIRS IS THE KINGDOM OF HEAVEN

The central theme of the Gospel is the kingdom of God. Jesus is the kingdom of God in person; he is Immanuel, God-with-us. And it is in the human heart that the kingdom, God's sovereignty, takes root and grows. The kingdom is at once both gift and promise. It has already been given to us in Jesus, but it has yet to be realized in its fullness. That is why we pray to the Father each day: "Thy kingdom come."

There is a close connection between poverty and evangelization, between the theme of the last World Youth Day—"Go therefore, and make disciples of all nations!" (Mt 28:19)—and the theme for this year: "Blessed are the poor in spirit, for theirs is the kingdom of heaven" (Mt 5:3). The Lord wants a poor Church that evangelizes the poor. When Jesus sent the Twelve out on mission, he said to them: "Take no gold, nor silver, nor copper in your belts, no bag for your journey, nor two tunics, nor sandals, nor a staff; for the laborers deserve their food" (Mt 10:9–10). Evangelical poverty is a basic condition for spreading the kingdom of God. The most beautiful and spontaneous expressions of joy which I have seen during my life were by poor people who had little to hold onto. Evangelization in our time will take place only as the result of contagious joy.

We have seen, then, that the Beatitude of the poor in spirit shapes our relationship with God, with material goods, and with the poor. The example and words of Jesus open our eyes to how much we need to be converted, so that the logic of *being more* will prevail over that of *having more*! The saints can best help us to understand the profound meaning of the Beatitudes. So the canonization of John Paul II, to be celebrated on the Second Sunday of Easter, will be an event marked by immense joy. He will be the great patron of the World Youth Days which he inaugurated and always supported. In the communion of saints he will continue to be a father and friend to all of you.

This month of April marks the thirtieth anniversary of the entrustment of the Jubilee Cross of the Redemption to the young. That symbolic act by John Paul II was the beginning of the great youth pilgrimage that has since crossed the five continents. The pope's words on that Easter Sunday in 1984 remain memorable: "My dear young people, at the conclusion of the Holy Year, I entrust to you the sign of this Jubilee Year: the cross of Christ! Carry it throughout the world as a symbol of the love of the Lord Jesus for humanity, and proclaim to everyone that it is only in Christ, who died and rose from the dead, that salvation and redemption are to be found."

Dear friends, the *Magnificat*, the Canticle of Mary, poor in spirit, is also the song of everyone who lives by the Beatitudes. The joy of the Gospel arises from a heart which, in its poverty, rejoices and marvels at the works of God, like the heart of Our Lady, whom all generations call "blessed" (cf. Lk 1:48). May Mary, mother of the poor and star of the new evangelization, help us to live the Gospel, to embody the Beatitudes in our lives, and to have the courage always to be happy.

—From the Vatican, January 21, 2014
Memorial of Saint Agnes, Virgin and Martyr

Message of Pope Francis for the Thirtieth World Youth Day, 2015

Blessed are the pure in heart,
for they shall see God. (Mt 5:8)

Dear Young Friends,

We continue our spiritual pilgrimage toward Kraków, where in July 2016 the next international World Youth Day will be held. As our guide for the journey we have chosen the Beatitudes. Last year we reflected on the Beatitude of the poor in spirit within the greater context of the Sermon on the Mount. Together we discovered the revolutionary meaning of the Beatitudes and the powerful summons of Jesus to embark courageously upon the exciting quest for happiness. This year we will reflect on the sixth Beatitude: "Blessed are the pure in heart, for they shall see God" (Mt 5:8).

THE DESIRE FOR HAPPINESS

The word *"blessed,"* or *"happy,"* occurs nine times in this, Jesus' first great sermon (cf. Mt 5:1–12). It is like a refrain reminding us of the Lord's call to advance together with him on a road which, for all its many challenges, leads to true happiness.

Dear young friends, this search for happiness is shared by people of all times and all ages. God has placed in the heart of every man and woman an irrepressible desire for happiness, for fulfillment. Have you not noticed that your hearts are restless, always searching for a treasure that can satisfy their thirst for the infinite?

The first chapters of the book of Genesis show us the splendid "beatitude" to which we are called. It consists of perfect communion with God, with others, with nature, and with ourselves. To approach God freely, to see him and to be close to him, was part of his plan for us from the beginning; his divine light was meant to illumine every human relationship with truth and transparency. In the state of original purity, there was no need to put on masks, to engage in ploys, or to attempt to conceal ourselves from one another. Everything was clear and pure.

When Adam and Eve yielded to temptation and broke off this relationship of trusting communion with God, sin entered into human history (cf. Gen 3). The effects were immediately evident within themselves and in their relationship with each other and with nature. And how dramatic the effects are! Our original purity was defiled. From that time on, we were no longer capable of closeness to God. Men and women began to conceal themselves, to cover their nakedness. Lacking the light which comes from seeing the Lord, they saw everything around them in a distorted fashion, myopically. The inner compass that had guided them in their quest for happiness lost its point of reference, and the attractions of power, wealth, possessions, and a desire for pleasure at all costs, led them to the abyss of sorrow and anguish.

In the psalms we hear the heartfelt plea that humanity makes to God: "What can bring us happiness? Let the light of your face shine on us, O Lord" (Ps 4:7). The Father, in his infinite goodness, responded to this plea by sending his Son. In Jesus, God has taken on a human face. Through his incarnation, life, death, and resurrection, Jesus frees us from sin and opens new and hitherto unimaginable horizons.

Dear young men and women, in Christ you find fulfilled your every desire for goodness and happiness. He alone can satisfy your deepest longings, which are so often clouded by deceptive worldly promises. As Saint John Paul II said: "He is the beauty to which you are so attracted; it is he who provokes you with that thirst for fullness that will not let you settle for compromise; it is he who urges you to shed the masks of a false life; it is he who reads in your hearts your most genuine choices, the choices that others try to stifle. It is Jesus who stirs in you the desire to do something great with your lives" (cf. Discourse at the Prayer Vigil at Tor Vergata, August 19, 2000: *Insegnamenti* XXIII/2, [2000], 212).

BLESSED ARE THE PURE IN HEART...

Let us now try to understand more fully how this blessedness comes about through purity of heart. First of all, we need to appreciate the biblical meaning of the word *heart*. In Hebrew thought, the heart is the center of the emotions, thoughts, and intentions of the human person. Since the Bible teaches us that God does not look to appearances, but to the heart (cf. 1 Sam 16:7), we can also say that it is from the heart that we see God. This is because the heart is really the human being in his or her totality as a unity of body and soul, in his or her ability to love and to be loved.

As for the definition of the word *pure*, however, the Greek word used by the evangelist Matthew is *katharos*, which basically means *clean, pure, undefiled*. In the Gospel we see Jesus reject a certain conception of ritual purity bound to exterior practices, one that forbade all contact with things and people (including lepers and strangers) considered impure. To the Pharisees who, like so many Jews of their time, ate nothing without first performing ritual ablutions and observing the many traditions associated with cleansing vessels, Jesus responds categorically: "There is nothing outside a man which by going into him can defile him; but the things which come out of a man are what defile him. For from within, out of the heart of man, come evil thoughts, fornication, theft, murder, adultery, coveting, wickedness, deceit, licentiousness, envy, slander, pride, foolishness" (Mk 7:15, 21–22).

In what, then, does the happiness born of a pure heart consist? From Jesus' list of the evils that make someone impure, we see that the question has to do above all with *relationships*. Each one of us must learn to discern what can "defile" his or her heart and to form his or her conscience rightly and sensibly, so as to be capable of "discerning the will of God, what is good and acceptable and perfect" (Rom

12:2). We need to show a healthy concern for creation, for the purity of our air, water, and food, but how much more do we need to protect the purity of what is most precious of all: *our heart and our relationships*. This "human ecology" will help us to breathe the pure air that comes from beauty, from true love, and from holiness.

Once I asked you the question: "Where is your treasure? In what does your heart find its rest?" (cf. Interview with Young People from Belgium, March 31, 2014). Our hearts can be attached to true or false treasures, they can find genuine rest or they can simply slumber, becoming lazy and lethargic. The greatest good we can have in life is our relationship with God. Are you convinced of this? Do you realize how much you are worth in the eyes of God? Do you know that you are loved and welcomed by him unconditionally, as indeed you are? Once we lose our sense of this, we human beings become an incomprehensible enigma, for it is the knowledge that we are loved unconditionally by God which gives meaning to our lives. Do you remember the conversation that Jesus had with the rich young man (cf. Mk 10:17–22)? The evangelist Mark observes that the Lord looked upon him and loved him (v. 21), and invited him to follow him and thus find true riches. I hope, dear young friends, that this loving gaze of Christ will accompany each of you throughout life.

Youth is a time of life when your desire for a love that is genuine, beautiful, and expansive begins to blossom in your hearts. How powerful is this ability to love and to be loved! Do not let this precious treasure be debased, destroyed, or spoiled. That is what happens when we start to use our neighbors for our own selfish ends, even as objects of pleasure. Hearts are broken and sadness follows upon these negative experiences. I urge you: do not be afraid of true love, the love that Jesus teaches us and that Saint Paul describes as "patient and kind." Paul says: "Love is not jealous or boastful; it is not arrogant or rude. Love does not insist on its own way; it is not irritable or resentful; it does not rejoice at wrong, but rejoices in the right. Love bears all things, believes all things, hopes all things, endures all things" (1 Cor 13:4–8).

In encouraging you to rediscover the beauty of the human vocation to love, I also urge you to rebel against the widespread tendency to trivialize love, making it banal and reducing it to its sexual aspect alone, deprived of its essential characteristics of beauty, communion, fidelity, and responsibility. Dear young friends, "in a culture of relativism and the ephemeral, many preach the importance of 'enjoying' the moment. They say that it is not worth making a lifelong commitment, making a definitive decision, 'forever,' because we do not know what tomorrow will bring. I ask you, instead, to be revolutionaries, I ask you to swim against the tide; yes, I am asking you to rebel against this culture that sees everything as temporary and that ultimately believes you are incapable of responsibility, that believes you are incapable of true love. I have confidence in you and I pray for you. Have the courage to 'swim against the tide.' And also have the courage to be happy" (Meeting with the Volunteers of the XXVIII World Youth Day, July 28, 2013).

You young people are brave adventurers! If you allow yourselves to discover the rich teachings of the Church on love, you will discover that Christianity does not consist of a series of prohibitions that stifle our desire for happiness, but rather a project for life capable of captivating our hearts.

...FOR THEY SHALL SEE GOD

In the heart of each man and woman, the Lord's invitation constantly resounds: "Seek my face!" (Ps 27:8). At the same time, we must always realize that we are poor sinners. For example, we read in the book of Psalms: "Who can climb the mountain of the Lord? Who shall stand in his holy place? The one who has clean hands and a pure heart" (Ps 24:3–4). But we must never be afraid or discouraged: throughout the Bible and in the history of each one of us we see that it is always God who takes the first step. He purifies us so that we can come into his presence.

When the prophet Isaiah heard the Lord's call to speak in his name, he was terrified and said: "Woe is me! I am lost; for I am a man of unclean lips" (Is 6:5). And yet the Lord purified him, sending to him an angel who touched his lips, saying: "Your guilt is taken away, and your sin is forgiven" (v. 7). In the New Testament, when on the shores of lake Genessaret Jesus called his first disciples and performed the sign of the miraculous catch of fish, Simon Peter fell at his feet, exclaiming: "Depart from me, for I am a sinful man, O Lord" (Lk 5:8). Jesus' reply was immediate: "Do not be afraid; henceforth you will be fishers of men" (v. 10). And when one of the disciples of Jesus asked him: "Lord, show us the Father, and we shall be satisfied," the Master replied: "He who has seen me has seen the Father (Jn 14:8–9).

The Lord's invitation to encounter him is made to each of you, in whatever place or situation you find yourself. It suffices to have the desire for "a renewed personal encounter with Jesus Christ, or at least an openness to letting him encounter you; I ask all of you to do this unfailingly each day" (cf. *Evangelii Gaudium*, 3). We are all sinners, needing to be purified by the Lord. But it is enough to take a small step toward Jesus to realize that he awaits us always with open arms, particularly in the sacrament of reconciliation, a privileged opportunity to encounter that divine mercy which purifies us and renews our hearts.

Dear young people, the Lord wants to meet us, to let himself "be seen" by us. "And how?" you might ask me. Saint Teresa of Avila, born in Spain five hundred years ago, even as a young girl said to her parents, "I want to see God." She subsequently discovered the way of *prayer* as "an intimate friendship with the One who makes us feel loved" (*Autobiography*, 8,5). So my question to you is this: "Are you praying?" Do you know that you can speak with Jesus, with the Father, with the Holy Spirit, as you speak to a friend? And not just any friend, but the greatest and most trusted of your friends! You will discover what one of his parishioners told the Curé of Ars: "When I pray before the tabernacle, I look at him, and he looks at me" (*Catechism of the Catholic Church*, 2715).

Once again I invite you to encounter the Lord by *frequently reading sacred scripture*. If you are not already in the habit of doing so, begin with the Gospels. Read a line or two each day. Let God's word speak to your heart and enlighten your path (cf. Ps 119:105). You will discover that God can be "seen" also *in the faces of your brothers and sisters,* especially those who are most forgotten: the poor, the hungry, those who thirst, strangers, the sick, those imprisoned (cf. Mt 25:31–46). Have you ever had this experience? Dear young people, in order to enter into the logic of the kingdom of Heaven, we must recognize that we are poor with the poor. A pure heart is necessarily one that has been stripped bare, a heart that knows how to bend down and share its life with those most in need.

Encountering God in prayer, the reading of the Bible, and the fraternal life will help you better to know the Lord and yourselves. Like the hearts of the disciples on the way to Emmaus (cf. Lk 24:13–35), your heart too will burn within you when you hear the Lord's voice. He will open your eyes to recognize his presence and to discover the loving plan he has for your life.

Some of you feel, or will soon feel, the Lord's call to married life, to forming a family. Many people today think that this vocation is "outdated," but that is not true! For this very reason, the ecclesial community has been engaged in a special period of reflection on the vocation and the mission of the family in the Church and the contemporary world. I also ask you to consider whether you are being called to the consecrated life or the priesthood. How beautiful it is to see young people who embrace the call to dedicate themselves fully to Christ and to the service of his Church! Challenge yourselves, and with a pure heart do not be afraid of what God is asking of you! From your "yes" to the Lord's call, you will become new seeds of hope in the Church and in society. Never forget: God's will is our happiness!

ON THE WAY TO KRAKÓW

"Blessed are the pure in heart, for they shall see God" (Mt 5:8). Dear young men and women, as you see, this Beatitude speaks directly to your lives and is a guarantee of your happiness. So once more I urge you: Have the courage to be happy!

This year we begin the final stage of preparations for the great gathering of young people from around the world for World Youth Day in Kraków in 2016. Thirty years ago Saint John Paul II instituted World Youth Days in the Church. The pilgrimage of young people from every continent under the guidance of the Successor of Peter has truly been a providential and prophetic initiative. Together let us thank the Lord for the precious fruits that these World Youth Days have produced in the lives of countless young people in every part of the globe! How many amazing discoveries have been made, especially the discovery that Christ is the Way, the Truth, and the Life! How many people have realized that the Church is a big and welcoming family! How many conversions, how many vocations have these gatherings produced! May the saintly pope, the Patron of World Youth Day, intercede on behalf of our pilgrimage toward his beloved Kraków. And may the maternal gaze of the Blessed Virgin Mary, full of grace, all-beautiful and all-pure, accompany us at every step along the way.

—*From the Vatican, January 31, 2015*
Memorial of Saint John Bosco

Message of Pope Francis
for the Thirty-first
World Youth Day, 2016

Blessed are the merciful,
for they shall obtain mercy. (Mt 5:7)

Dear Young People,

We have come to the last stretch of our pilgrimage to Kraków, the place where we will celebrate the thirty-first World Youth Day next year in the month of July. We are being guided on this long and challenging path by Jesus' words taken from the Sermon on the Mount. We began our journey in 2014 by meditating together on the first Beatitude: "Blessed are the poor in spirit, for theirs is the kingdom of heaven" (Mt 5:3). The theme for 2015 was: "Blessed are the pure in heart, for they shall see God" (Mt 5:8). During the year ahead, let us allow ourselves to be inspired by the words: "Blessed are the merciful, for they shall obtain mercy" (Mt 5:7).

THE JUBILEE OF MERCY

With this theme, the Kraków 2016 World Youth Day forms part of the Holy Year of Mercy and so becomes a Youth Jubilee at world level. It is not the first time that an international youth gathering has coincided with a Jubilee Year. Indeed, it was during the Holy Year of the Redemption (1983/1984) that Saint John Paul II first called on young people from around the world to come together on Palm Sunday. Then, during the Great Jubilee of the year 2000, over two million young people from about 165 countries gathered in Rome for the fifteenth World Youth Day. I am sure that the Youth Jubilee in Kraków will be, as on those two previous occasions, one of the high points of this Holy Year!

Perhaps some of you are asking: What is this Jubilee Year that is celebrated in the Church? The scriptural text of Leviticus 5 can help us to understand the meaning of a "jubilee" for the people of Israel. Every fifty years they heard the sounding of a trumpet (*jobel*) calling them (*jobil*) to celebrate a holy year as a time of reconciliation (*jobal*) for everyone. During that time they were to renew their good relations with God, with their neighbors and with creation, all in a spirit of gratuitousness. This fostered, among other things, debt forgiveness, special help for those who had fallen into poverty, an improvement in interpersonal relations, and the freeing of slaves.

Jesus Christ came to proclaim and bring about the Lord's everlasting time of grace. He brought good news to the poor, freedom to prisoners, sight to the blind and freedom to the oppressed (cf. Lk 4:18–19). In Jesus, and particularly in his Paschal Mystery, the deeper meaning of the jubilee is fully realized. When the Church proclaims a jubilee in the name of Christ, we are all invited to experience a wonderful time of grace. The Church must offer abundant signs of God's presence and closeness and reawaken in people's hearts the ability to look to the essentials. In particular, this Holy Year of Mercy is "a time for the Church to rediscover the meaning of the mission entrusted to her by the Lord on the day of Easter: to be a sign and an instrument of the Father's mercy" (Homily at First Vespers of Divine Mercy Sunday, April 11, 2015).

MERCIFUL LIKE THE FATHER

The motto for this Extraordinary Jubilee is "Merciful like the Father" (cf. *Misericordiae Vultus*, 13). This fits in with the theme of the next World Youth Day, so let us try to better understand the meaning of divine mercy.

The Old Testament uses various terms when it speaks about mercy. The most meaningful of these are *hesed* and *rahamim*. The first, when applied to God, expresses God's unfailing fidelity to the covenant with his people whom he loves and forgives forever. The second, *rahamim*, which literally means "entrails," can be translated as "heartfelt mercy." This particularly brings to mind the maternal womb and helps us understand that God's love for his people is like that of a mother for her child. That is how it is presented by the prophet Isaiah: "Can a mother forget her infant, be without tenderness for the child of her womb?

Even should she forget, I will never forget you" (Is 49:15). Love of this kind involves making space for others within ourselves and being able to sympathize, suffer, and rejoice with our neighbors.

The biblical concept of mercy also includes the tangible presence of love that is faithful, freely given, and able to forgive. In the following passage from Hosea, we have a beautiful example of God's love, which the prophet compares to that of a father for his child: "When Israel was a child I loved him; out of Egypt I called my son. The more I called them, the farther they went from me...Yet it was I who taught Ephraim to walk, who took them in my arms; I drew them with human cords, with bands of love; I fostered them like one who raises an infant to his cheeks...I stooped to feed my child" (Hos 11:1–4). Despite the child's wrong attitude that deserves punishment, a father's love is faithful. He always forgives his repentant children. We see here how forgiveness is always included in mercy. It is "not an abstract idea, but a concrete reality with which he reveals his love as of that of a father or a mother, moved to the very depths out of love for their child...It gushes forth from the depths naturally, full of tenderness and compassion, indulgence and mercy" (*Misericordiae Vultus*, 6).

The New Testament speaks to us of divine mercy (*eleos*) as a synthesis of the work that Jesus came to accomplish in the world in the name of the Father (cf. Mt 9:13). Our Lord's mercy can be seen especially when he bends down to human misery and shows his compassion for those in need of understanding, healing and forgiveness. Everything in Jesus speaks of mercy. Indeed, he himself *is* mercy.

In chapter 15 of Luke's Gospel we find the three parables of mercy: the lost sheep, the lost coin, and the parable of the prodigal son. In these three parables we are struck by God's joy, the joy that God feels when he finds and forgives a sinner. Yes, it is God's joy to forgive! This sums up the whole of the Gospel. "Each of us, each one of us, is that little lost lamb, the coin that was mislaid; each one of us is that son who has squandered his freedom on false idols, illusions of happiness, and has lost everything. But God does not forget us; the Father never abandons us. He is a patient Father, always waiting for us! He respects our freedom, but he remains faithful forever. And when we come back to him, he welcomes us like children into his house, for he never ceases, not for one instant, to wait for us with love. And his heart rejoices over every child who returns. He is celebrating because he is joy. God has this joy, when one of us sinners goes to him and asks his forgiveness" (*Angelus*, September 15, 2013).

God's mercy is very real and we are all called to experience it firsthand. When I was seventeen years old, it happened one day that, as I was about to go out with friends, I decided to stop into a church first. I met a priest there who inspired great confidence, and I felt the desire to open my heart in confession. That meeting changed my life! I discovered that when we open our hearts with humility and transparency, we can contemplate God's mercy in a very concrete way. I felt certain that, in the person of that priest, God was already waiting for me even before I took the step into that church. We keep looking for God, but God is there before us, always looking for us, and he finds us first.

Maybe one of you feels something weighing on your heart. You are thinking: I did this, I did that...Do not be afraid! God is waiting for you! God is a father and he is always waiting for us! It is so wonderful to feel the merciful embrace of the Father in the sacrament of reconciliation, to discover that the confessional is a place of mercy, and to allow ourselves to be touched by the merciful love of the Lord who always forgives us!

You, dear young man, dear young woman, have you ever felt the gaze of everlasting love upon you, a gaze that looks beyond your sins, limitations, and failings and continues to have faith in you and to look upon your life with hope? Do you realize how precious you are to God, who has given you everything out of love? Saint Paul tells us that "God proves his love for us in that, while we were still sinners, Christ died for us" (Rom 5:8). Do we really understand the power of these words?

I know how much the World Youth Day cross means to all of you. It was a gift from Saint John Paul II and has been with you at all your world meetings since 1984. So many changes and real conversions have taken place in the lives of young people who have encountered this simple bare cross! Perhaps you have asked yourselves the question: What is the origin of the extraordinary power of the cross? Here is the answer: the cross is the most eloquent sign of God's mercy! It tells us that the measure of God's love for humanity is to love without measure! Through the cross we can touch God's mercy and be touched by that mercy! Here I would recall the episode of the two thieves crucified with Jesus. One of them is arrogant and does not admit that he is a sinner. He mocks the

Lord. The other acknowledges that he has done wrong; he turns to the Lord saying: "Jesus, remember me when you come into your kingdom." Jesus looks at him with infinite mercy and replies: "Today you will be with me in Paradise" (cf. Lk 23:32, 39–43). With which of the two do we identify? Is it with the arrogant one who does not acknowledge his own mistakes? Or is it with the other, who accepts that he is in need of divine mercy and begs for it with all his heart? It is in the Lord, who gave his life for us on the cross, that we will always find that unconditional love which sees our lives as something good and always gives us the chance to start again.

THE AMAZING JOY OF BEING INSTRUMENTS OF GOD'S MERCY

The word of God teaches us that "it is more blessed to give than to receive" (Acts 20:35). That is why the fifth Beatitude declares that the merciful are blessed. We know that the Lord loved us first. But we will be truly blessed and happy only when we enter into the divine "logic" of gift and gracious love, when we discover that God has loved us infinitely in order to make us capable of loving like him, without measure. Saint John says: "Beloved, let us love one another, because love is of God; everyone who loves is begotten by God and knows God. Whoever is without love does not know God, for God is love ... In this is love: not that we have loved God, but that he loved us and sent his Son as expiation for our sins. Beloved, if God so loved us, we also must love one another" (1 Jn 4:7–11).

After this very brief summary of how the Lord bestows his mercy upon us, I would like to give you some suggestions on how we can be instruments of this mercy for others.

I think of the example of Blessed Pier Giorgio Frassati. He said, "Jesus pays me a visit every morning in Holy Communion, and I return the visit in the meager way I know how, visiting the poor." Pier Giorgio was a young man who understood what it means to have a merciful heart that responds to those most in need. He gave them far more than material goods. He gave himself by giving his time, his words, and his capacity to listen. He served the poor very quietly and unassumingly. He truly did what the Gospel tells us: "When you give alms, do not let your left hand know what your right is doing, so that your almsgiving may be secret" (Mt 6:3–4). On the day before his death, while he was gravely ill, Pier Giorgio was giving directions on how his friends in need should be helped. At his funeral, his family and friends were stunned by the presence of so many poor people whom they didn't know. They had been befriended and helped by the young Pier Giorgio.

I always like to link the Gospel Beatitudes with Matthew 25, where Jesus presents us with the works of mercy and tells us that we will be judged on them. I ask you, then, to rediscover the corporal works of mercy: to feed the hungry, give drink to the thirsty, clothe the naked, welcome the stranger, assist the sick, visit the imprisoned, and bury the dead. Nor should we overlook the spiritual works of mercy: to counsel the doubtful, teach the ignorant, admonish sinners, comfort the sorrowful, forgive offenses, patiently bear with troublesome people, and pray to God for the living and the dead. As you can see, mercy does not just imply being a "good person" nor is it mere sentimentality. It is the measure of our authenticity as disciples of Jesus, and of our credibility as Christians in today's world.

If you want me to be very specific, I would suggest that for the first seven months of 2016 you choose a corporal and a spiritual work of mercy to practice each month. Find inspiration in the prayer of Saint Faustina, a humble apostle of Divine Mercy in our times:

"Help me, O Lord,

... that my eyes may be merciful, so that I will never be suspicious or judge by appearances, but always look for what is beautiful in my neighbors' souls and be of help to them;

... that my ears may be merciful, so that I will be attentive to my neighbors' needs, and not indifferent to their pains and complaints;

... that my tongue may be merciful, so that I will never speak badly of others, but have a word of comfort and forgiveness for all;

... that my hands may be merciful and full of good deeds;

... that my feet may be merciful, so that I will hasten to help my neighbor, despite my own fatigue and weariness;

... that my heart may be merciful, so that I myself will share in all the sufferings of my neighbor" (Diary, 163).

The Divine Mercy message is a very specific life plan because it involves action. One of the most obvious works of mercy, and perhaps the most difficult to put into practice, is to forgive those who have offended us, who have done us wrong, or whom we consider to be enemies. "At times how hard it seems to forgive! And yet pardon is the instrument placed into our fragile hands to attain serenity of heart. To let go of anger, wrath, violence, and revenge is a necessary condition for living joyfully" (*Misericordiae Vultus*, 9).

I meet so many young people who say that they are tired of this world being so divided, with clashes between supporters of different factions and so many wars, in some of which religion is being used as justification for violence. We must ask the Lord to give us the grace to be merciful to those who do us wrong. Jesus on the cross prayed for those who had crucified him: "Father, forgive them, they know not what they do" (Lk 23:34). Mercy is the only way to overcome evil. Justice is necessary, of course, but by itself it is not enough. Justice and mercy must go together. How I wish that we could join together in a chorus of prayer, from the depths of our hearts, to implore the Lord to have mercy on us and on the whole world!

KRAKÓW IS EXPECTING US!

Only a few months are left before we meet in Poland. Kraków, the city of Saint John Paul II and Saint Faustina Kowalska, is waiting for us with open arms and hearts. I believe that Divine Providence led us to the decision to celebrate the Youth Jubilee in that city which was home to those two great apostles of mercy in our times. John Paul II realized that this is the time of mercy. At the start of his pontificate, he wrote the encyclical *Dives in Misericordia*. In the Holy Year 2000 he canonized Sister Faustina and instituted the feast of Divine Mercy, which now takes place on the Second Sunday of Easter. In 2002 he personally inaugurated the Divine Mercy Shrine in Kraków and entrusted the world to Divine Mercy, in the desire that this message would reach all the peoples of the earth and fill their hearts with hope: "This spark needs to be lighted by the grace of God. This fire of mercy needs to be passed on to the world. In the mercy of God the world will find peace and mankind will find happiness!" (Homily at the Dedication of the Divine Mercy Shrine in Kraków, August 17, 2002).

Dear young people, at the Shrine in Kraków dedicated to the merciful Jesus, where he is depicted in the image venerated by the people of God, Jesus is waiting for you. He has confidence in you and is counting on you! He has so many things to say to each of you . . . Do not be afraid to look into his eyes, full of infinite love for you. Open yourselves to his merciful gaze, so ready to forgive all your sins. A look from him can change your lives and heal the wounds in your souls. His eyes can quench the thirst that is deep in your young hearts, a thirst for love, for peace, for joy, and for true happiness. Come to him and do not be afraid! Come to him and say from the depths of your hearts: "Jesus, I trust in You!" Let yourselves be touched by his boundless mercy, so that in turn you may become apostles of mercy by your actions, words, and prayers in our world, wounded by selfishness, hatred, and so much despair.

Carry with you the flame of Christ's merciful love—as Saint John Paul II said—in every sphere of your daily life and to the very ends of the earth. In this mission, I am with you with my encouragement and prayers. I entrust all of you to Mary, Mother of Mercy, for this last stretch of the journey of spiritual preparation for the next World Youth Day in Kraków. I bless all of you from my heart.

—From the Vatican, August 15, 2015
Solemnity of the Assumption of the Blessed Virgin Mary

Message of Pope Francis
for the Thirty-second
World Youth Day, 2017

"The Mighty One has done great things for me" (Lk 1:49)

Dear Young Friends,

Here we are, on the road again, following our great meeting in Kraków, where we celebrated the thirty-first World Youth Day and the Jubilee for Young People as part of the Holy Year of Mercy. We took as our guides Saint John Paul II and Saint Faustina Kowalska, the apostles of divine mercy, in order to offer a concrete response to the challenges of our time. We had a powerful experience of fraternity and joy, and we gave the world a sign of hope. Our different flags and languages were not a reason for rivalry and division, but an opportunity to open the doors of our hearts and to build bridges.

At the conclusion of the Kraków World Youth Day, I announced the next stop in our pilgrimage, which, with God's help, will bring us to Panama in 2019. On this journey we will be accompanied by the Virgin Mary, whom all generations call blessed (cf. Lk 1:48). This new leg of our journey picks up from the one that preceded it, centered on the Beatitudes, and invites us to press forward. I fervently hope that you young people will continue to press forward, not only cherishing the *memory* of the past, but also with *courage* in the present and *hope* for the future. These attitudes were certainly present in the young Mary of Nazareth and are clearly expressed in the themes chosen for the three coming World Youth Days. This year (2017) we will reflect on the faith of Mary, who says in the Magnificat: *"The Mighty One has done great things for me"* (*Lk* 1:49). The theme for next year (2018)—*"Do not be afraid, Mary, for you have found favor with God"* (Lk 1:30)—will lead us to meditate on the courageous charity with which the Virgin welcomed the message of the angel. The 2019 World Youth Day will be inspired by the words: *"I am the servant of the Lord. May it be done to me according to your word"* (Lk 1:38), Mary's hope-filled reply to the angel.

In October 2018, the Church will celebrate the Synod of Bishops on the theme: *Youth, Faith, and Vocational Discernment*. We will talk about how you, as young people, are experiencing the life of faith amid the challenges of our time. We will also discuss the question of how you can develop a life project by discerning your personal vocation, whether it be to marriage in the secular and professional world, or to the consecrated life and priesthood. It is my hope that the journey toward the World Youth Day in Panama and the process of preparation for the synod will move forward in tandem.

OUR AGE DOES NOT NEED
YOUNG PEOPLE WHO ARE "COUCH-POTATOES"

According to Luke's Gospel, once Mary has received the message of the angel and said "yes" to the call to become the mother of the Savior, she sets out in haste to visit her cousin Elizabeth, who is in the sixth month of her pregnancy (cf. 1:36, 39). Mary is very young; what she has been told is a great gift, but it also entails great challenges. The Lord has assured her of his presence and support, yet many things remain obscure in her mind and heart. Yet Mary does not shut herself up at home or let herself be paralyzed by fear or pride. Mary is not the type that, to be comfortable, needs a good sofa where she can feel safe and sound. She is no couch potato! (cf. Address at the Vigil, Kraków, July 30, 2016). If her elderly cousin needs a hand, Mary does not hesitate, but immediately sets off.

It was a long way to the house of Elizabeth, about 150 kilometers. But the young woman from Nazareth, led by the Holy Spirit, knew no obstacles. Surely, those days of journeying helped her to meditate on the marvelous event of which she was a part. So it is with us, whenever we set out on pilgrimage. Along the way, the events of our own lives come to mind. We learn to appreciate their meaning and we discern our vocation, which then becomes clear in the encounter with God and in service to others.

THE MIGHTY ONE HAS DONE GREAT THINGS FOR ME

The meeting of the two women, one young and the other elderly, is filled with the presence of the Holy Spirit and charged with joy and wonder (cf. Lk 1:40–45). The two mothers, like the children they bear, practically dance for joy. Elizabeth, impressed by Mary's faith, cries out: "Blessed is she who believed that there would be a fulfillment of what was spoken to her by the Lord" (v. 45). One of the great gifts that the Virgin received was certainly that of faith. Belief in God is a priceless gift, but one that has to be received. Elizabeth blesses Mary for this, and she in turn responds with the song of the Magnificat (cf. Lk 1:46–55), in which we find the words: "The Mighty One has done great things for me" (v. 49).

Mary's is a revolutionary prayer, the song of a faith-filled young woman conscious of her limits yet confident in God's mercy. She gives thanks to God for looking upon her lowliness and for the work of salvation that he has brought about for the people, the poor and the humble. Faith is at the heart of Mary's entire story. Her song helps us to understand the mercy of the Lord as the driving force of history, the history of each of us and of all humanity.

When God touches the heart of a young man or woman, that person becomes capable of doing tremendous things. The "great things" that the Almighty accomplished in the life of Mary speak also to our own journey in life, which is not a meaningless meandering, but a pilgrimage that, for all its uncertainties and sufferings, can find its fulfillment in

God (cf. *Angelus*, August 15, 2015). You may say to me: "But Father, I have my limits, I am a sinner, what can I do?" When the Lord calls us, he doesn't stop at what we are or what we have done. On the contrary, at the very moment that he calls us, he is looking ahead to everything we can do, all the love we are capable of giving. Like the young Mary, you can allow your life to become a means for making the world a better place. Jesus is calling you to leave your mark in life, your mark on history, both your own and that of so many others (cf. Address at the Vigil, Kraków, July 30, 2016).

BEING YOUNG DOES NOT MEAN
BEING DISCONNECTED FROM THE PAST

Mary was little more than an adolescent, like many of you. Yet in the Magnificat, she echoes the praises of her people and their history. This shows us that being young does not mean being disconnected from the past. Our personal history is part of a long trail, a communal journey that has preceded us over the ages. Like Mary, we belong to a people. History teaches us that, even when the Church has to sail on stormy seas, the hand of God guides her and helps her to overcome moments of difficulty. The genuine experience of the Church is not like that of a flash mob, where people agree to meet, do their thing, and then go their separate ways. The Church is heir to a long tradition which, passed down from generation to generation, is further enriched by the experience of each individual. Your personal history has a place within the greater history of the Church.

Being mindful of the past also helps us to be open to the unexpected ways in which God acts in us and through us. It also helps us to be open to being chosen as a means by which God brings about his saving plan. As young people, you too can do great things and take on fuller responsibilities, if only you recognize God's mercy and power at work in your lives.

I would like to ask you some questions. How do you "save" in your memory the events and experiences of your life? What do you do with the facts and the images present in your memory? Some of you, particularly those hurt by certain situations in life, might want to "reset" your own past, to claim the right to forget it all. But I would like to remind you that there is no saint without a past, or a sinner without a future. The pearl is born of a wound in the oyster! Jesus, by his love, can heal our hearts and turn our lives into genuine pearls. As Saint Paul said, the Lord can show his power through our weakness (cf. 2 Cor 12:9).

Yet our memories should not remain crammed together, as in the memory of a hard drive. Nor can we archive everything in some sort of virtual "cloud." We need to learn how to make past events a dynamic reality on which to reflect and to draw lessons and meaning for the present and the future. This is no easy task, but one that is necessary for discovering the thread of God's love running through the whole of our life.

Many people say that young people are distracted and superficial. They are wrong! Still, we should acknowledge our need to reflect on our lives and direct them toward the future. To have a past is not the same as to have a history. In our life we can have plenty of *memories*, but how many of them are really a part of our *memory*? How many are significant for our hearts and help to give meaning to our lives? In social media, we see faces of young people appearing in any number of pictures recounting more or less real events, but we don't know how much of all this is really "history," an experience that can be communicated and endowed with purpose and meaning. Television is full of "reality shows" that are not real stories, but only moments passed before a television camera by characters living from day to day, without a greater plan. Don't let yourselves be led astray by this false image of reality! Be the protagonists of your history; decide your own future.

HOW TO REMAIN CONNECTED, FOLLOWING THE EXAMPLE OF MARY

It is said of Mary that she treasured all these things and pondered them in her heart (cf. Lk 2:19, 51). This unassuming young woman of Nazareth teaches us by her example to preserve the memory of the events of our lives but also to put them together and reconstruct the unity of all the fragments that, put together, can make up a mosaic. How can we learn to do this? Let me offer you some suggestions.

At the end of each day, we can stop for a few minutes to remember the good times and the challenges, the things that went well and those that went wrong. In this way, before God and before ourselves, we can express our gratitude, our regrets, and our trust. If you wish, you can also write your thoughts down in a notebook as a kind of spiritual journal. This means praying in life, with life, and about life, and it will surely help you to recognize the great things that the Lord is doing for each of you. As Saint Augustine said, we can find God in the vast fields of our memory (cf. *Confessions*, X, 8, 12).

Reading the Magnificat, we realize how well Mary knew the word of God. Every verse of her song has a parallel in the Old Testament. The young mother of Jesus knew the prayers of her people by heart. Surely her parents and her grandparents had taught them to her. How important it is for the faith to be passed down from one generation to another! There is a hidden treasure in the prayers that past generations have taught us, in the lived spirituality of ordinary people that we call *popular piety*. Mary inherits the faith of her people and shapes it into a song that is entirely her own, yet at the same time is the song of the entire Church, which sings it with her. If you, as young people, want to sing a Magnificat all your own, and make your lives a gift for humanity as a whole, it is essential to connect with the historical tradition and the prayer of those who have gone before you. To do so, it is important to be familiar with the Bible, God's word, reading it daily and letting it speak to your lives, interpreting everyday events in the light of what the Lord says to you in the sacred scriptures. In prayer and in the prayerful reading of the Bible (*lectio divina*), Jesus will warm your hearts and illumine your steps, even in the dark moments of life (cf. Lk 24:13–35).

Mary also teaches us to live "eucharistically," that is, to give thanks and praise, and not to fixate on our problems and difficulties alone. In the process of living, today's prayers become tomorrow's reasons for thanksgiving. In this way, your participation in Holy Mass and the occasions when you celebrate the sacrament of reconciliation will be both a high point and new beginning. Your lives will be renewed each day in forgiveness and they will become an act of perennial praise to the Almighty. "Trust the memory of God . . . his memory is a heart filled with tender compassion, one that rejoices in erasing in us every trace of evil" (cf. *Homily at Mass, World Youth* Day, Kraków, July 31, 2016).

We have seen that the Magnificat wells up in Mary's heart at the moment when she meets her elderly cousin Elizabeth. With her faith, her keen gaze, and her words, Elizabeth helps the Virgin to understand more fully the greatness of what God is accomplishing in her and the mission that he has entrusted to her. But what about you? Do you realize how extraordinarily enriching the encounter between the young and the elderly can be? How much attention do you pay to the elderly, to your grandparents? With good reason you want to "soar," your heart is full of great dreams, but you need the wisdom and the vision of the elderly. Spread your wings and fly, but also realize that you need to rediscover your roots and to take up the torch from those who have gone before. To build a meaningful future, you need to know and appreciate the past (cf. *Amoris Laetitia*, 190, 193). Young people have strength, while the elderly have memory and wisdom. As Mary did with Elizabeth, look to the elderly, to your grandparents. They will speak to you of things that can thrill your minds and fill your hearts.

CREATIVE FIDELITY FOR BUILDING THE FUTURE

It is true that you are still young and so it can be hard for you to appreciate the importance of tradition. But know that this is not the same as being traditionalists. No! When Mary in the Gospel says: "The Mighty One has done great things for me," she means to say that those "great things" are not over, but are still happening in the present. It is not about the distant past. Being mindful of the past does not mean being nostalgic or remaining attached to a certain period of history, but rather being able to acknowledge where we have come from, so that we can keep going back to essentials and throwing ourselves with creative fidelity into building the future. It would be problematic and ultimately useless to cultivate a paralyzing memory that makes us keep doing the same things in the same way. It is a gift of God to see how many of you, with your questions, dreams, and uncertainties, refuse to listen to those who say that things cannot change.

A society that values only the present tends to dismiss everything inherited from the past, as, for example, the institutions of marriage, consecrated life, and priestly mission. These end up being seen as meaningless and outdated forms. People think it is better to live in "open" situations, going through life as if it were a reality show, without aim or purpose. Don't let yourselves be deceived! God came to enlarge the horizons of our life in every direction. He helps us to give due value to the past so as to better build a future of happiness. Yet this is possible only if we have authentic experiences of love, which help us concretely to discern the

Lord's call and to respond to it. For only that can bring us true happiness.

Dear young people, I entrust our journey towards Panama, together with the process of preparation for the next Synod of Bishops, to the maternal intercession of the Blessed Virgin Mary. I ask you to keep in mind two important anniversaries in 2017: the three-hundredth anniversary of the finding of the image of Our Lady of Aparecida in Brazil and the centenary of the apparitions in Fatima, Portugal, where, God willing, I plan to make a pilgrimage this coming May. Saint Martin of Porres, one of the patron saints of Latin America and of the 2019 World Youth Day, in going about his humble daily duties, used to offer the best flowers to Mary, as a sign of his filial love. May you too cultivate a relationship of familiarity and friendship with Our Lady, entrusting to her your joys, your worries, and your concerns. I assure you that you will not regret it!

May the maiden of Nazareth, who in the whole world has assumed a thousand names and faces in order to be close to her children, intercede for all of us and help us to sing of the great works that the Lord is accomplishing in us and through us.

—From the Vatican, February 27, 2017
Memory of Saint Gabriel of Our Lady of Sorrows

FINAL REFLECTIONS

Looking Back, Looking Ahead

First Vespers on the Solemnity of Mary, Mother of God, and *Te Deum* in Thanksgiving for the Past Year

Homily, Vatican Basilica, December 31, 2016

As another year draws to an end, let us pause before the manger and express our gratitude to God for all the signs of his generosity in our life and our history, seen in countless ways through the witness of those people who quietly took a risk. A gratitude that is no sterile nostalgia or empty recollection of an idealized and disembodied past, but a living memory, one that helps to generate personal and communal creativity because we know that God is with us. God is with us.

Let us pause before the manger to contemplate how God has been present throughout this year and to remind ourselves that every age, every moment, is the bearer of graces and blessings. The manger challenges us not to give up on anything or anyone. To look upon the manger means to find the strength to take our place in history without complaining or being resentful, without closing in on ourselves or seeking a means of escape, without seeking shortcuts in our own interest. Looking at the manger means recognizing that the times ahead call for bold and hopefilled initiatives, as well as the renunciation of vain self-promotion and endless concern with appearances.

Looking at the manger means seeing how God gets involved by involving us, making us part of his work, inviting us to welcome the future courageously and decisively.

Looking at the manger, we see Joseph and Mary, their young faces full of hopes and aspirations, full of questions. Young faces that look to the future conscious of the difficult task of helping the God-Child to grow. We cannot speak of the future without reflecting on these young faces and accepting the responsibility we have for our young; more than a responsibility, the right word would be debt, yes, the debt we owe them. To speak of a year's end is to feel the need to reflect on how concerned we are about the place of young people in our society.

We have created a culture that idolizes youth and seeks to make it eternal. Yet, at the same time, paradoxically, we have condemned our young people to have no place in society, because we have slowly pushed them to the margins of public life, forcing them to migrate or to beg for jobs that no longer exist or fail to promise them a future. We have preferred speculation to dignified and genuine work that can allow young people to take an active part in the life of society. We expect and demand that they be a leaven for the future, but we discriminate against them and "condemn" them to knock on doors that for the most part remain closed.

We are asked to be different from the innkeeper in Bethlehem who told the young couple: "There is no room here." There was no room for life, there was no room for the future. Each of us is asked to take some responsibility, however small, for helping our young people to find, here in their land, in their own country, real possibilities for building a future. Let us not be deprived of the strength of their hands, their minds, and their ability to prophesy the dreams of their ancestors (cf. Jl 2:28). If we wish to secure a future worthy of our young people, we should do so by basing it on true inclusion: one that provides work that is worthy, liberating, creative, and participatory (cf. Address at the Conferral of the Charlemagne Prize, May 6, 2016).

Looking at the manger challenges us to help our young people not become disillusioned by our own immaturity, but to spur them on so that they can be capable of dreaming and fighting for their dreams, capable of growing and becoming fathers and mothers of our people.

As we come to the end of this year, we do well to contemplate the God-Child! Doing so invites us to return to the sources and roots of our faith. In Jesus, faith becomes hope; it becomes a leaven and a blessing. "With a tenderness which never disappoints, but is always capable of restoring our joy, Christ makes it possible for us to lift up our heads and to start anew" (*Evangelii Gaudium*, 3).

Letter of Pope Francis to Young People

on the Occasion of the Presentation of the Preparatory Document
of the Fifteenth Ordinary General Assembly
of the Synod of Bishops

My Dear Young People,

I am pleased to announce that in October 2018 a Synod of Bishops will take place to treat the topic: "Young People, the Faith, and Vocational Discernment." I wanted you to be the center of attention, because you are in my heart. Today, the Preparatory Document is being presented, a document that I am also entrusting to you as your "compass" on this synodal journey.

I am reminded of the words that God spoke to Abraham: "Go from your country and your kindred and your father's house to the land that I will show you" (Gen 12:1). These words are now also addressed to you. They are words of a father who invites you to "go," to set out toward a future that is unknown but one that will surely lead to fulfillment, a future toward which he himself accompanies you. I invite you to hear God's voice resounding in your heart through the breath of the Holy Spirit.

When God said to Abram, "Go!" what did he want to say? He certainly did not ask Abram to distance himself from his family or withdraw from the world. Abram received a compelling invitation, a challenge, to leave everything and go to a new land. What is this "new land" for us today, if not a more just and friendly society which you, young people, deeply desire and wish to build for the entire earth?

But unfortunately, today, "Go!" also has a different meaning, namely, that of abuse of power, injustice, and war. Many among you are subjected to the real threat of violence and forced to flee your native land. Their cry goes up to God, like that of Israel when the people were enslaved and oppressed by Pharaoh (cf. Ex 2:23).

I would also remind you of the words that Jesus once said to the disciples who asked him: "Teacher... where are you staying?" He replied, "Come and see" (Jn 1:38). Jesus looks at you and invites you to go with him. Dear young people, have you noticed this look toward you? Have you heard this voice? Have you felt this urge to undertake this journey? I am sure that, despite the noise and confusion seemingly prevalent in the world, this call continues to resonate in the depths of your heart so as to open it to joy in its fullness. This will be possible to the extent that, with the guidance of experts, you learn how to undertake a journey of discernment to discover God's plan in your life. Even when the journey is uncertain and you fall, God, rich in mercy, will extend his hand to pick you up.

In Kraków, at the opening of the last World Youth Day, I asked you several times: "Can we change things?" And you shouted: "Yes!" That shout came from your young and youthful hearts, which do not tolerate injustice and cannot bow to a "throw-away culture" nor give in to the globalization of indifference. Listen to the cry arising from your inner selves! Even when you feel, like the prophet Jeremiah, the inexperience of youth, God encourages you to go where he sends you: "Do not be afraid,... because I am with you to deliver you" (Jer 1:8).

A better world can be built also as a result of your efforts, your desire to change, and your generosity. Do not be afraid to listen to the Spirit who proposes bold choices; do not delay when your conscience asks you to take risks in following the Master. The Church also wishes to listen to your voice, your sensitivities, and your faith; even your doubts and your criticism. Make your voice heard, let it resonate in communities and let it be heard by your shepherds of souls. Saint Benedict urged the abbots to consult, even with the young, before any important decision, because "the Lord often reveals to the younger what is best" (*Rule of Saint Benedict*, III, 3).

Such is the case even in the journey of this synod. My brother bishops and I want even more to "work with you for your joy" (2 Cor 1:24). I entrust you to Mary of Nazareth, a young person like yourselves, whom God beheld lovingly, so she might take your hand and guide you to the joy of fully and generously responding to God's call with the words: "Here I am" (cf. Lk 1:38).

> With paternal affection,
> FRANCIS
> *Given at the Vatican, January 13, 2017*

JUN -- 2018